Create Your Own

Family Originals

**Over 500 Ways to Preserve Everyday Humor,
Family Lore and Significant Milestones**

Celebrate your stories!

Luci and Lucy

We shall not cease from exploration
And the end of all our exploring
Will be to arrive where we started
And know the place for the first time.

— T.S. Eliot
Four Quartets

ISBN 0-9764222-0-4

Family Originals is the trademark of LuCreative Enterprises, LLC.

Any trademarks or servicemarks used herein are the property of
their respective registered owners and, except for "Family Originals,"
no claim thereto is made by the authors or publishers of this work.

Ordering information is available at
www.familyoriginals.com.

Book design by
David Hunt Creative, Inc.
Columbia, South Carolina
davidhuntcreative.com

First Edition
Printed in the United States of America

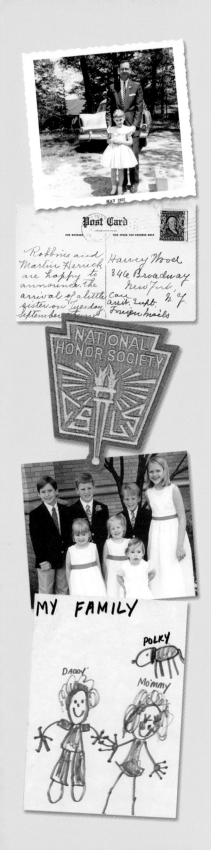

Table of Contents

What is a Family Original?

Throughout this book we refer to *Family Originals,*™ our term for the highly personal handiwork that honors everyday humor, family lore or significant milestones of life. A *Family Original*™ can be anything that celebrates and passes along unique stories and memories from your life, your family's and your friends'. The form is easy to share with family and friends who were part of that history and with future generations whose legacy you preserve.

Your *Family Original*™ may be as simple as a photocopied letter or as involved as a photographic record of a family member's school years. The pages that follow are filled with easy ideas and inspiring stories about real people and their *Family Originals.*™ Open this book to any page for engaging possibilities. Other people's stories will trigger your own and, once you begin, you'll find the process starts telling its own story.

A *Family Original*™ is also an extraordinary gift to those who mean the most. As you turn the pages, you'll find very special gift ideas that celebrate family and honor a beloved individual. The best gift of all, however, may be your own recollections, triggered by making a *Family Original.*™

Fam-i-ly Orig-i-nal™ \'fam-(ə-)lē\ \ə-'rij- ən-'l\ (2004):   *n.* **1**: a packaged memory **2**: gift for loved ones **3**: journey in self-discovery **4**: reflection and connection **5**: tangible emotions **6**: process and product **7**: past-present-future **8**: history in the making **9**: legacy **10**: surprise and discovery **11**: ongoing story **12**: celebration through preservation *Family Original*™ *adj.* **1**: unique **2**: meaningful **3**: personal **4**: delightful **5**: inspired and inspiring **6**: selective **7**: whimsical **8**: comforting **9**: touching **10**: thoughtful **11**: fun **12**: creative **13**: engaging **14**: lasting **15**: ageless **16**: timeless

Fear Factors

The longest distance between two points is intention and action.

"I'm having such a hard time getting started," said Sharon, mother of four grown children, an accomplished woman in her own right. "I have all these boxes of photos and memorabilia I want to organize for my children and for myself, for that matter. If I don't, what will happen to the memories?"

Sharon is the voice of hundreds of baby boomers. She has lived long enough to know how quickly time moves, how important history is, and how essential it is to do her part to preserve it. But she never quite gets around to it.

Sharon's voice could also belong to a new mother overwhelmed by countless pictures and mounting memorabilia from this exciting new chapter in her life. She, too, wants to preserve these fleeting moments for her child and for herself and her husband. With daily demands consuming her time, organizing and preserving these family stories seems like a luxury at this point, so she, too, misses the opportunity.

Finally, Sharon's voice could be coming from hundreds of members of the greatest generation, now retired, with—it would seem—all the time in the world to preserve the stories. Many have moved their boxes of memories from one location to another, fully intending to record their lessons of a lifetime. Thus, they put all their precious history at risk.

Given the value we all place on family memories, why is there such resistance to preserving them? We think there are five looming fear factors that lock us into procrastination. In this chapter, we'll address each factor and replace it with a motivating action plan.

Fear Factor Volume

Most of us have a lot of "stuff" to begin with. Added to our own memorabilia are boxes of memorabilia one or two generations removed. No wonder the starting point seems overwhelming.

Along with the sheer volume of family material is another, equally powerful force…the emotional challenge. Anyone who has come across saved notes, letters or photographs knows the power they hold. The question becomes one of stopping right then and reading them, or putting them in a special place to read at another time. If you do stop then to read them, you know how they can transport you to another time and place. Some times and places are easier to revisit than others; some are deeply painful. In the midst of a demanding present tense, we sometimes resist the vulnerability our memorabilia connotes.

Finally, there are practical dimensions. "Getting all this stuff out" can create a mess. It is therefore normal to resist introducing more chaos into our full, hectic lives.

Don't despair! There is good news: you don't have to do it all at once. This book will show you how to break down memorabilia into manageable bites, how to quickly select and focus on the pieces of your story that matter most. You'll read how others got beyond the seemingly overwhelming volume, emotion and interruption of ordering memorabilia. Inspired by their stories, you'll see new options and easy ways to chronicle your memories.

Fear Factor Creativity

The word "creativity" can frighten, but in truth, your memories have already been created. Your mission is to preserve them. As you turn the pages of this book, you'll be introduced to idea after idea from real people working with memorabilia similar to yours.

You'll also be amazed at the number of resources out there to help you organize your story. For example, if you choose, you can send your recipes to a specialty service that will create your family cookbook for you. The same is true of your photographs and other memorabilia. By relying on an experienced service to produce the end product, you can transform your assorted items into albums, collages, memory boxes, and quilts. These and other simpler treatments you can do on your own are a lifesaver as they become your signature gift solutions for birthdays, anniversaries, holidays, graduations, weddings, and retirement.

Most important, you'll find yourself on a journey of self-discovery, a journey that will take on a life of its own. One step will lead to the next.

Once you start going through your memorabilia, you will be amazed at the way it "declares itself" and shows you how to tell the stories. We guarantee it and have real life examples to prove it.

Fear Factor Expense

Like the time factor, cost can create resistance, and no doubt about it—some ideas in this book are more expensive than others. However, many of them are free. The pages that follow are filled with low-cost ideas. You can start with an inexpensive idea such as a personal photo calendar. Later you can implement a more expensive idea such as professionally duplicating and framing heritage photographs.

Here's the best way to think about cost. What you are preserving is priceless. You cannot put a dollar value on the memories of a lifetime or the pleasure you will get from preserving those stories. Think of the legacy you are passing on to future generations. Commercials for credit cards such as MasterCard® differentiate between what can be bought and what is "priceless." For a one-time cost, you are insuring priceless history will be preserved for generations.

Preserving your history isn't always free, but all the money in the world can't buy it back once it's been lost or destroyed.

Fear Factor Time

Even when you know what you'd like to do with that memorabilia, the time commitment can be scary. The natural anxiety intensifies when you have a deadline such as a loved one's birthday or anniversary or graduation. Instead of looking at this milestone as a motivator, you become stressed by it.

Creating *Family Originals*™ can be time consuming, but it does not have to be more time consuming than other kinds of gift giving. Think of the time you've spent over the years searching for just the right gift. Even more frustrating is time you invest without finding the right gift. In contrast, when you make a *Family Original*,™ you are giving something of yourself to those you love and thus honoring the priority of loved ones.

The key to dealing with the time factor is three-fold:

1. Make the most of available time. For example, put a scrapbook together two pages at a time. Smock a child's dress while you're waiting in the dentist's office. Keep a tablet and pen handy to record children's expressions.

2. The most time-consuming step is the first. Once you start, the time involved becomes secondary. When your *Family Original*™ is finished, you will be gratified and inspired to do more.

3. Have a great time as you take time to create *Family Originals*.™

Family stories are always one generation away from extinction. Take time to preserve time.

Fear Factor Family

Someone once said, "How you feel about your family is a complicated thing." We all know how true that is. However, family history is *your* history.

In writing this book we met one woman who, on a whim, visited an aunt she had not seen in years. We'll let her tell you the rest.

"That visit changed my life. She gave me a box of memorabilia her own children had shown no interest in. I started reading letters and became awed by what my ancestors had done. I vowed I'd be a better person because of the lessons these people from previous generations taught me. Sometimes I can't believe how close I came to never knowing this...my own history. Once I started reading, I saw myself as a steward of this information. I duplicated excerpts for other family members, and they have become equally affected."

Revisiting the past from your current perspective can enhance the present and the future. In going back we often go forward.

A friend keeps a copy of a Ziggy® cartoon on her refrigerator where Ziggy, chin on hand, sits under this balloon: "I can't believe my life is based on a true story."

We challenge you to embrace the true stories of your life...settings, characters and episodes. This book will show you how, story after story, idea after idea. You are in for an extraordinary treat!

Advice, Wisdom & Family Lore

Photographs

Recipes

Journals, Letters & e-mail

Decorative Objects & Décor

★ NEWSPAPER CLIPPINGS ★

Textiles & Needlework

EXPRESSIONS

Music

And

Dance

HOME ★ MOVIES & TAPES

You are surrounded by the "raw materials" of your personal history. Revisit them now with a new perspective as the starting point for your own *Family Originals.*™

Photographs

You have meaningful photographs that no one else has. Here are some ways you can use them in *Family Originals.*™

Quick Tips for Getting Started

Chances are, your photographs are all over your house...in an envelope, a drawer, correspondence you've saved, the back of a shelf, boxes, closets, stacks. Don't despair! Instead, try this easy 1-2-3 approach: start small; sort big; give back.

1. Start small.
Begin with photos in just one drawer, one box or one envelope.

2. Group big.
As you look at your pictures, you'll be surprised at the way groupings emerge. There are no incorrect ways to group. Many categories even overlap. Here are some of our favorites.

August 1999

February 1999

- Chapters in Our Family's Life (holidays, big events, travel)
- Chapters in My Spouse's Life (years before we met, hobbies and interests, our courtship, friends)
- People Special to Us (friends, family members)
- Same Picture Over Time (different people in their caps and gowns; the "going away" picture from different weddings; various people blowing out their birthday candles)
- Big Events (birthdays, graduations, weddings, baptisms, retirement, family reunions)
- Animals
- Vacations
- Holidays
- "Who are these people?"
  (This is your assortment of "orphan photos." Everyone has them.)
- Negatives
- Duplicates

These sorted photos now need a temporary home. Choose your containers—envelopes, boxes, folders—and label them. Later you can sort your pictures into smaller categories.

3. Give back.
Think of your photographs as potential gifts, especially those pictures no one else has. You can start by selecting 12 favorite photos of a special person. All you have to do is take those photos to a copy shop and have a personalized calendar made. BINGO! You've just turned a dozen pictures into a meaningful gift.

A bigger project might appeal to you for a loved one's milestone birthday or anniversary (such as the 30th). Play with the corresponding number.
- Arrange 30 pictures of the honoree in a collage or even an album.
- Present 30 pictures chronologically.
- List 30 attributes of the honoree (funny, athletic, kind, creative, eccentric, handy) and group pictures by attribute.
- Write 30 birthday wishes or 30 moments of a lifetime. Add corresponding photos.

Imagine the look on that person's face when your extraordinary gift is opened.

Year in Review

Use pictures to make your own informative, fun holiday card like this. It's so easy. Just make a collage. Then color copy it at a copy shop, and share your year with family and friends.

Photographs

Go forward and backward in time and pose. In the 1960s, the brothers on the bottom mimicked
the humor and creativity of the brothers on the top, their grandfather and great uncle.
What fun photographs in your family albums beg replication by the current generation?

Ideas!

- Purchase a simple brass plaque and attach it to the front of a heritage photograph to tell its story.

- Abandon order and replicate real life by creating a spontaneous "refrigerator gallery." Take pictures from a drawer or closet, and display them on the refrigerator or a bulletin board. Periodically change the exhibit. As you do, move the pictures from the refrigerator into an album, and note their significance. Pay no attention to chronology or theme. "Moments of a Lifetime" is a great title for this entertaining **Family Original**.

- A simple way to connect generations through photographs is to look for activities, organizations and locations that repeatedly appear. For example, you may have photographs of scouting through the generations or different generations attending the same camp. That type of collage is an easy focus for a **Family Original**.

- Consider turning favorite photographs into a quilt. Office supply stores and craft stores carry iron-on kits for transferring photographs onto fabric. Look in the Yellow Pages or on the Web under "photo quilts" to tap resources that will create your quilt for you; you simply supply the photos. Pillows are another possibility and make great wedding, graduation and Christmas gifts.

- School pictures are a universal way to display history. If you're lucky, the dates are already printed on the pictures. You can easily frame this version of the family's story. You can also make a quilt of school pictures. Another idea is to make a 12-page album for a family member. Add the corresponding school pictures and your memories, and entitle the gift "A Dozen Years in a Special Life."

The Unidentified Salute

"I'm looking at this wonderful picture taken 50 years ago," says Mary Heath Etheridge, "but I can't identify all the members of my troop. I wish I'd thought to write those names on the back at the time, but, of course, in the second grade, I didn't think about that."

The moral of the story is this: Take the time at the time to identify the people in your photographs.

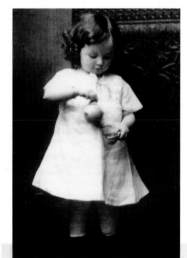

Take favorite photos to a print shop to explore ways to create note paper, invitations and holiday cards. They blend the past and the present.

A birthday brunch, and you're invited
We want you there—we're all excited
With family we'll be reunited
As birthday candles are ignited!

Abingdon's her place of birth.
To mark her 90 years on earth
It is her choice for the location
Of her upcoming celebration.

August 31's the day; 1914's the year
Of the birth of this person we all hold so dear:
Daughter of Judge F. B. and Ruby Clark Hutton,
The picture shows she was "cute as a button!"

Although most of her playmates have gone to their rest,
Now from her heart it's her birthday request
To be with their children to reflect and remember
So please mark this date: it's the fourth of September.

Martha Washington is the setting;
We hope you will not be regretting;
Hosts Hutton, Bill, Lucie, and Sally
Have promised the Inn they would give a tally,
So please let us know—one way or the other—
If you can help us honor our Mother.

BIRTHDAY BRUNCH

honoring

Ruby Hutton Barron

Martha Washington Inn

September 4, 2004

11 o'clock

RSVP by August 30, 2004

1-800-489-7324
leggleston@bellsouth.net

no gifts, please

Photographs

General Photography Tips

1. Focus on the subject and avoid background intrusions such as a tree appearing to come out of someone's head.

2. When you have a single subject in a picture, your picture will be more interesting if the subject is just off-center. For a group picture, it is fine to center the crowd.

3. When you are on vacation, it's sometimes fun to get pictures of yourself at famous places to prove you were there. In addition, sometimes a person standing next to a vista can indicate size and scale.

4. By turning the camera, you can vary the photographs so that you get both horizontal and vertical pictures. Different viewpoints add interest and variety to your photo collection.

5. If you have an automatic camera, be sure to avoid bright light behind the subject. Such bright light, called backlight, throws off the camera's light meter and causes the subject to become a shadow.

6. If you cannot avoid backlighting, be sure to use a flash fill even outdoors to light the subject.

7. Film comes in different film speeds indicated by the ISO number on the box. For general use, 400 speed is practical for both outdoor and indoor flash photography. Action pictures need a speed of 400 or higher to avoid blurring. For outdoor photography, 200 speed or lower is fine.

8. Casual pictures are great fun, but sometimes you should gather the group for a posed shot just so you make sure to include everyone.

9. Plan pictures ahead of an event. Make a list of people you want to include in your photographs. If you are taking pictures of your child's school performance, be sure to get a close-up of the child before and after the event. Also plan staged pictures to go with the spontaneous shots.

10. Keep camera, extra film and extra batteries handy. Many of the best pictures are those candid camera ones.

Digital Photography Tips

Digital cameras are changing the way we take photographs.

1. Digital cameras allow the instant satisfaction of seeing the image on the back of the camera.

2. Seeing images immediately allows you to select the best shots and delete the others.

3. Digital photography allows you to crop and improve the images with computer programs designed for editing images. For example, red eye can be eliminated easily.

4. Digital photography allows you to cut-and-paste several images together using graphics programs.

5. Digital photography is less cumbersome. You can store digital memory cards until ready to print. Memory cards are less bulky than film and store large numbers of images.

6. Digital memory cards allow you to immediately download your images to your computer and view your pictures.

7. If you make a request when you take your regular film to be processed, many photo developers will produce a CD at a nominal cost. The CD is another way to store image files. By getting a CD when you develop your film, you can still use your film camera and e-mail your pictures to friends and family.

8. Programs are available to organize and index your digital images on your computer. Some of these programs can produce a simple Web site or an album. You can purchase these programs at computer and electronics stores or on the Web.

9. Photographs can be printed from digital images with your home computer and printer. It is important to use high-quality photo paper and high-quality ink in your printer.

10. Many photo developing stores have machines that allow you to print pictures from your digital memory cards. The price is comparable to ordering pictures online from the numerous digital photography developing sites on the Web.

Rare and prized collections such as this one can be professionally duplicated — photos, frame and mat. The result will be that all interested family members can have their own *Family Original.*™ Start by going to a professional photo shop or framer. On the back of each framed collection, attach a sheet of paper identifying the individuals and any relevant information you can add such as birth and death dates.

Braggin' Rights and Christmas Cards

It's undeniable! Grandparents are indeed proud of their precious grandchildren. Over 50 years ago, this creative holiday card combined Christmas greetings and "grandparental pride."

Today we have digital photography and e-mail to instantly share photographs with friends and relatives. Still, the yearly holiday card with photograph is an easy way to capture the chapters of our lives, reflect the styles and fashions over the years, and tell your family story.

What can you do with the extra photographs from a trip? Turn them into a collage you can enjoy every time you walk by it. Better still, follow the example of Caroline Crosswell: create a collage as a gift for others who shared your travels. It's the perfect way to tell a story of friendship and adventure.

Photographs

Texas-sized Portrait Susan Murphey has a compelling photograph in her house that most Texans would buy in an antique store and claim as their very own. This picture is of a larger-than-life, cigar-smoking cowboy. The best part for Susan, however, is that this prototype of the old West is her grandfather, the youngest man to serve as a sheriff in Texas. He later became a Texas Ranger. To ensure the integrity of this information for future generations, Susan typed this story on a card and attached it to the back of the photograph. She can also duplicate this unique photograph for members of her family.

Duplicate heritage photographs for family members; identify the people and attach information on the back.

Instead of the "Over the Hill" party theme, use a childhood picture on that 40th birthday party invitation. Not only does it add a personal note, but it also brings back memories and generates smiles from the guests. You can use this invitation idea for any milestone birthday, or you can apply the concept to anniversary party invitations, engagement party invitations, or family reunion announcements.

Faces from the Forties

Although portraits and snapshots were not as prevalent in the 1940s as they are today, many families have a few studio photographs of their children. This portrait of the Hamiltons lined up in stair-step order is typical of the era. The sour look on each child's face leads one to believe the photographer had not yet learned to get his subjects to say, "Cheese!"

Create an instant gallery with one of your tables. Any home improvement store can cut the glass to fit the top of your table. You can label pictures in the collection if you'd like. When you get tired of it, move those pictures to an album. During the holidays, consider displaying seasonal pictures taken through the years. If possible, date them.

Which is it?... a collection of memories or the entertainment for a gathering of family or friends? It's both. Albums provide hours of pleasure and enjoyment. They also document real moments in life.

Cheese Soufflé

Six or seven average slices of
bread (cut crust from bread)
¾ pound Sharp or medium sharp
Cheese grated (add 1 teaspoon salt and
1 teaspoon dry mustard to grated cheese)
Four eggs (Five if eggs are small)
2½ cup milk

Butter Casserole — Then cut
bread slices in squares and
butter.
Place one layer of buttered
bread squares in casserole.
Now put layer of grated cheese
mixture — add another layer
of bread squares — and layer
of cheese mixture —
Beat eggs well and add
milk and mix well — now
[...] over
[...] in
[...] at least
[...] days
[...] make
[...] next day

Recipes

*Recipes have traveled through time, distance and
generations to nourish family members and their
memories. Your family's recipes have, too.*

*Recipes are more than a list of ingredients and cooking
instructions. They convey love, nourishment, history and
community. Use them to create Family Originals.*

Ideas!

- Is there a special recipe that has become part of family gatherings through the generations? Frame that treasured hand-written recipe, note its origin, and list the occasions where it has been served.

- Create a collage or album of photographs from occasions where a treasured recipe has been served. The original recipe can be the center of the collage or the title page of the album. Label and date the occasions.

- Collect your family favorites in a cookbook. This is a fabulous gift for family members and friends. Entitle it "Seasoned with Love." You do not have to produce the cookbook yourself. Resources such as local copy shops and printers can help you. You can also find numerous resources on the Web. Simply type "family cookbooks" into any search engine.

- Are you looking for a personal way to honor your mother? Collect and duplicate her recipes, and entitle the collection "I Remember Mama."

- Expand your Family Cookbook by including favorite menus, corresponding photographs and family blessings.

- Here's a great Christmas present for family and friends. Create a recipe book featuring holiday stories and memories. You can organize the recipes around menus for family gatherings or in traditional cookbook chapters (appetizers, salads, etc.).

Mommy's Little Helper

A handprint is a memory snapshot. That's why every time young Verd Anna Cunningham helped her mother prepare a recipe, her mother traced her hand and dated the handprinted page in the cookbook. When Verd Anna graduated from high school, her mother put together a collection of the handprinted recipes for Verd Anna and entitled the collection *Mommy's Little Helper*.

Brides, Babies and Cheese Straws

Dorothy Herlong Warr's famous cheese straws have been part of family celebrations for four generations. Her original handwritten recipe now hangs in the kitchen of her granddaughter, Meg Christian. When Meg looks at the recipe, she not only thinks about her grandmother, but she also thinks of rehearsal parties, baptisms and holiday gatherings from Clayton, Alabama, to Princeton, New Jersey. What recipe in your family links celebrations and generations?

Recipes

Ideas!

- Here's a new twist on a proven idea. For someone "just going out into the world" or for a new bride, host a Recipe Shower. Ask guests to bring a special family recipe and the essential dish, pan or gadget for preparing it. For entertainment, ask each guest to tell the recipe's story. Videotape the presentation. The tape becomes an abbreviated "Cooking School" for the new cook.

- Supper clubs can take on a life of their own. If you're part of such a group, have fun recording your history in a collection of mobile memories. All you really need to get started is an album. At each gathering, the host couple will record the evening's highlights. Those highlights might include menus or recipes, photographs or stories. The album then goes to the next host couple. Think of the fun the group will have looking at the mobile collection at each gathering.

- If you're not in a supper club, why not start one? Everyone can share favorite recipes and tell their stories.

- For the sports enthusiast, collect your tailgating recipes and memories in an album. Incorporate the name of your sport in the title of your collection. For example, football fans could entitle their cookbook "Football Seasons and Seasonings."

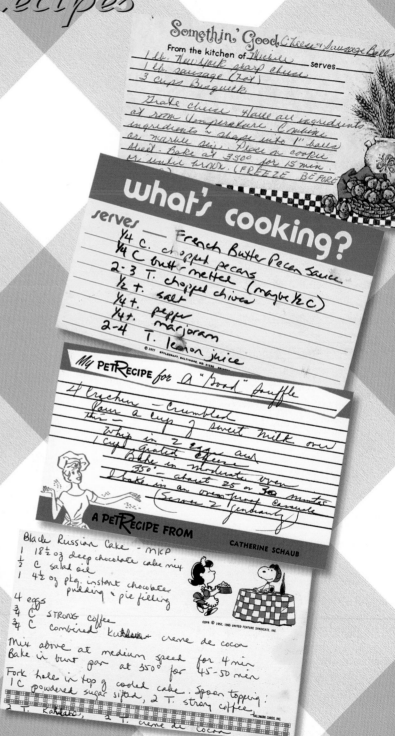

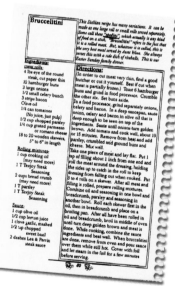

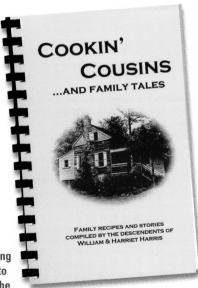

Missie McCarty

Old Fashioned Bread with Starter

1/4 cup sugar
1 cup flour *
1/2 cup water
3/4 cup water
2 tablespoons sugar
1 teaspoon salt
1/4 cup Mazola oil
3 1/4 cups flour *

The night before making bread put starter in a large bowl and add the first 3 ingredients (sugar, flour and water). Mix and stir until smooth. Cover with a wet cloth and let rise all night. The next morning stir well and take out 1/2 cup of this sponge mixture. Put in a wide mouth jar, seal and put in the refrigerator for the next bread making.

To the remainder of sponge add next 5 ingredients (water, sugar, salt, oil and flour). Make this into smooth dough by mixing and kneading sponge right in the same bowl. Set aside. Cover to rise until double — 3 to 5 hours.

over

For Starters

Dan McCarty never shops the bread aisle at the grocery store. The reason? He grew up with the aroma of his mother's homemade bread baking in the oven. Now that aroma permeates his own home.

"To make this bread, you *have to have* some of Mrs. McCarty's starter," explains Dan's wife, Missie. "Once when Dan accidentally let the bread starter expire, he drove from Texas to Louisiana to get this essential ingredient."

Although no one lives by bread alone, Dan's bread-making ritual sustains a family connection and feeds his family's spirit. What are the rituals that feed your family's spirit?

Try This...

Which of your recipes are in demand? List them here. Note their origin and story. You have just started your **Family Original** cookbook.

_____

_____

_____

_____

_____

_____

_____

_____

_____

_____

_____

_____

_____

_____

_____

Spedini — Don't Leave Home Without It.

Recipes can be a unifying symbol and activity at a family reunion. Just ask Olivia Fertitta and her daughter Vicki West. When they make their signature family spedini it is an all-day project.

Once every five years, family members come from California, Las Vegas, Texas and Louisiana to gather in a large hotel for a family reunion. However, they don't leave the spedini at home. Instead, it travels with every branch in frozen form.

A highlight of the reunion is the spedini dinner on Saturday night. The kitchen staff clears the freezers and cooks the spedini for the 400 family members who gather in the ballroom. That Saturday night, spedini takes on a whole new meaning. Because each family unit has come to the reunion with a special version of the signature item, there are subtle changes among the casseroles; there is great fun and laughter guessing whose spedini is whose.

What is your signature family recipe?

The Harris family used a publishing company they found on the Web to compile their family cookbook. The committee for this treasured collection of recipes and stories included Inger Harris, Molly McCue, Marty McCue Nimmons, and Dotty Harris Zazworsky.

"In the Hole He Goes!"

Family expressions and mis-statements remind us of the ties that bind. Such is the case the day Jake Barker told his parents he had been "*indicted* into the Beta Club." That announcement obviously filled his parents with pride and amusement.

Think about the words and descriptions children you know have coined or misused to make sense of life's mysteries and complexities; those expressions can inspire a wonderful anthology of meaningful stories.

"Whose Idea Was This?"

EXPRESSIONS

"In the Hole He Goes"

Five-year-old Margaret Robinson, a Methodist, attended church with her Baptist relatives one Sunday morning when a baptism took place. This was a first for her, so later that afternoon she worked out a way to make sense of it. When her mother overheard Margaret in her room, she could not resist peeking in.

Margaret had filled a mixing bowl with water. She was picking up one of her paper dolls when her mother overheard her say with great confidence: **"I baptize thee in the name of the Father, and of the Son, and in the hole he goes!"** With that, the paper doll was officially immersed. This classic story belongs in a collection of family expressions.

"Whose Idea Was This?"

When young Jim Barron's family went to a restaurant (a big treat), he would look around and ask, "Whose idea was this?" In Jim's mind, the one who had thought of the outing deserved all the credit. His father thought the more appropriate question was, "Who's paying for this?"

Jim is now a father himself. However, when the family gathers for any successful outing, someone always asks, **"Whose idea was this?"** This remark confirms the family's highest approval.

Ideas!

Your family expressions and mis-statements are unique shortcuts in family communication. That's why they are appealing material for **Family Originals.**

- Create your own dictionary of family expressions and mis-statements. Supplement your collection with photos of the originators, preferably at the time in life the expressions surfaced. A collection like this is a great welcome-to-the-family gift for a new in-law.

- Incorporate family expressions in your toast to the bride and groom at the rehearsal dinner. Be sure to give a copy of the toast to the couple for their wedding album.

- Use expressions in a skit at a family reunion. Videotape the production.

- Sometimes nicknames are stories in themselves. As part of a family album, include nicknames and tell their story.

- For a family get-together, let everyone tell their favorite expression originated by another family member; tape the storytelling.

"I'm Not Seeing You"

"I Went In All Together"

Try This...

What are your family expressions and mis-statements? Jot them down right now. Note who originated each expression. You have just completed step one of a great collection of family stories.

_____
_____
_____
_____
_____
_____
_____
_____
_____
_____
_____
_____
_____
_____
_____
_____

EXPRESSIONS

"I'm Not Seeing You"

It's a well-known fact that obedience is not always appealing, and this was sometimes the case with young Laura Haas. Instead of refusing outright to obey her mother, however, Laura would simply turn away and politely announce, "I'm not seeing you."

To this day the Haas family uses Laura's words for any request that lacks appeal. It actually backfired on Laura when she became a teenager and wanted to stay out past curfew. Her mother could have said, "You know the rules." Instead, she turned away from her daughter and said, "I'm not seeing you," which automatically softened a negative response but made the point.

"I Went In All Together"

Four-year-old Robin Jackson was swimming in Lake Marion with his mother and some of her friends the day he uttered immortal words. His mother had helped him swim out to a float about 20 yards from the shore, encouraging him to dive into the water. He dove in several times and was very proud of himself. His mother was just as proud.

Upon returning to shore, she bragged to Robin's grandmother, "You should have seen your grandson diving into the water today."

Impressed, Robin's grandmother quickly responded, "Oh, no, Robin—did you go head first?"

Looking puzzled, Robin replied, **"I went in all together."**

That story instantly became a family favorite. Several years later, after Robin's little brother Richard was born, Robin's mother filled in a contest blank attached to a new baby carrier. Winners of the contest would have their story published in Art Linkletter's "Kids Still Say the Darndest Things." The grand prize also included $1000 in merchandise from Condon's Department Store in Charleston, where the baby carrier had been purchased.

Months went by; then one day the telephone rang. It was the sponsor of the contest calling to tell Mrs. Jackson she had won. Everyone was excited, especially the children. Robin's immortal words had brought the family "fame and fortune," but his best gift has been the priceless story that lives on.

"Music is the one art we all have inside... All of us have had the experience of hearing a tune from childhood and having that melody evoke a memory or a feeling. The music we hear early on tends to stay with us all our lives."

— Fred Rogers
The World According to Mister Rogers

Music And Dance

Ideas!

- Remember going public with music and dance, whether you were talented or not? Think about piano recitals, dance recitals, choir performances, band concerts, school musicals, and local talent shows. What are your personal show stoppers? Record them in writing or on tape. Entitle your memories "Encore Performances."

- Did you ever take music lessons? If so, create a journal, album or collage around your memories. For example, if you took piano lessons, answer the following questions in recollections, photographs, programs, and sheet music:
  - Who introduced you to the instrument?
  - Who were your music teachers?
  - What pieces did you learn "by heart" and even perform in public?

- What did taking lessons teach you about discipline, persistence and commitment? How have these experiences influenced your appreciation of music?

- What are your memories of professional performances?
  - The Symphony
  - Broadway Shows
  - Operas
  - Musical Revues
  - Country Music Concerts
  - Jazz Performances
  - Bluegrass Festivals
  - Rock Concerts
  - Musical Theatre

- Attention parents. What are YOUR memories of children practicing their musical instruments in the home? How did they throw your household "off-key"?

They're Playing Our Song

When once asked how she and her husband met, Lucy Lewis immediately responded, "Tchaikovsky brought us together, but Beethoven tied us forever. It was the summer of 1967, and we were at a party for mutual friends who were getting married. On the way home, a concerto by Tchaikovsky was playing on the radio. It was one of my favorites. When I mentioned that, I got a surprising response," she recalls.

"'I didn't know you liked classical music,' Eric said. 'If I were to purchase season tickets to the symphony next year, would you be interested in going with me?'

"I'd already decided I'd be very interested in going out with him again, so 'Yes!' was my answer almost before he finished the question. In September we had our first symphony date. The evening's concert featured Beethoven's spectacular Ninth Symphony. The performance was absolutely wonderful.

"For Christmas that year, Eric surprised me with a recording of Beethoven's Ninth. When we became engaged a year later, I selected the 'Ode to Joy' from Beethoven's Ninth to walk down the aisle. Now 35 years and three children later when we hear this masterpiece, we say, 'They're playing our song.'"

Music can lead to the beginning of a relationship, provide a gift for a special occasion, and call to mind a meaningful story such as this one.

What is your signature song and, more important, what is its story?

A Keyboard for the Score Board

The band starts playing; the team rushes out; the crowd goes wild! Every time Pete Dempsey sees that happen, he remembers a day many years ago when two priests came to his house. The priests sat down at the piano and played a tune they had written.

A short time later that tune was adopted as the "Notre Dame Fight Song." Pete is proud to say it was first played for his family on his grandfather's Steinway. That heirloom piano now sits in Pete's home and continues to tell significant stories.

What stories do your musical instruments tell?

Music And Dance

A Talent, A Livelihood, A Legacy

"Memories of my mother conjure up her fabulous musical talent," says Kathryn Egan Stout. "Although raising nine children provided little time for herself, she found spare moments to 'bang away' at her beloved Steinway. The piece played was a great indication of her current mood. Wrapped into this amazing God-given talent were perfect pitch, exciting rhythm and, in her later years, a gift for composing her own music.

"As Mother aged, widowed, remarried, and enjoyed her 22 grandchildren and great grands, her music flourished.

"I often thought of how all this joy needed to be preserved…our family favorites, her children's rhythms, her beloved tribute songs written for friends' birthdays. Her legacy must live on!

"Thus, I proposed to her the idea of recording her music. My persistence that she fly to Atlanta from Green Bay and spend some time in a recording studio led to a lasting and loving family memory.

"That first tape was a huge hit. Mother loved giving that tape to friends, and my siblings loved the memories it rekindled. Two subsequent tapes followed before her death.

"As I listen now to these tapes," continues Kathryn, "I have her with me and feel her mood, her talent, her energy. A mother myself, I now understand how music sustained her through raising nine kids."

Highland Park Presbyterian Church
Presents
1986
TAP & BALLET RECITAL

"Miss Jean" Bleakley

Toe Tappin' Memories

"Celebrate the child in you, and live your dreams." advises Cindy Dempsey.

"That's what I did when I started taking tap-dancing lessons at age 40. We showcased our accomplishments each year in a recital. Once a class member had performed for 10 years, however, she got to *star* in the recital.

"When I reached this milestone, I soloed in a boa and a crown, and I have the video to prove it."

"I have been singing all my life," says Jay Barron, "but started playing the guitar when I realized that people who just sit in their rooms singing to themselves are often considered 'crazy people.' On the other hand, people who strum simple chords while singing to themselves in their rooms are sometimes called 'performing artists.'

"I decided to do this CD because I had a notebook of songs that always felt like an unfinished project. I also felt a need to have something I could share. Having produced a CD, even one as primitive as mine, is my tangible accomplishment, like some people want to write a book or hang their watercolors in a gallery.

"The best part of this project was receiving the final copies in the mail. I nervously opened one, put it in the player, lay on the floor and listened all the way through, grimacing at each wrong note, of which there were plenty. I was so proud of it, and I have enjoyed sharing it."

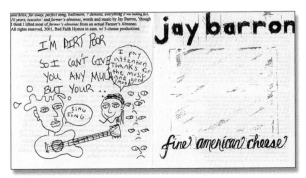

Try This...

Who are the musicians in your family? List them here along with your musical associations. You have just "noted" your musical "family tree." Contact several people on your list to brainstorm ways to preserve your family talent.

_____

_____

_____

_____

_____

_____

_____

_____

Ideas!

- Were you ever part of a musical group — a band, chorus, singing group, or musical family? What pictures, programs and memories can you collect in an album?

- Create a CD with the music that tells your story. For example, a bride and groom can combine the music that defines their courtship. The CD cover can be a collage of photographs of the couple.

- If you have home movies and videotapes of performances, transfer them to DVD. Then add your recollections as a vocal overlay. Duplicate the DVD as a gift for the people who were part of the stories.

HOME★MOVIES

& TAPES

You have always had a starring role in the story of your life. Some moments may have even been immortalized on film. For every family that has made home movies and videotapes, it's time to get those award-winning performances into the distribution network of your family. Everyone will enjoy the reruns.

Out of Africa

In every family there are characters who travel to faraway places and become "citizens of the world." That's the kind of person Katherine Hopkins' grandfather was. As early as 1936 he traveled extensively in Africa. What is even more amazing is his record of those adventures. The family not only has 16mm movies of their grandfather's African travels; they also have his letters.

Katherine is creating an extraordinary *Family Original*™ by splicing readings from the letters into the footage they have now transferred onto videotape. Her son John, who majored in drama at Northwestern, is reading select entries. The project thus links four generations.

Playing and Saying

"I grew up with music in the home… the music of my mother at the piano," says Sally LaBadie. "I wanted to be able to hear this music forever, so I arranged for Mother to make a tape in a local recording studio. Mother, who had been playing the piano for more than 80 years, made the selections based on the music and memories of her life. One side was hymns; the other was show tunes and pop music. The tape was Mother's Christmas present that year to her children, grandchildren and closest friends."

Her mother's recording inspired Sally's own gift idea for family members. She arranged for her mother to be videotaped recalling her reasons for each musical selection. "That Christmas was so special," Sally recalls. "First everyone opened their audiotape from Mother. Then they opened their videotapes. That afternoon we sat down as a family and watched the videotape, three generations enjoying the music and storytelling. I believe it was equally gratifying for Mother because the next year she made another recording…this time of her holiday favorites."

I Do Two

"Although home video cameras are commonplace today, 50 years ago movie cameras were a rare possession in the home," says Pete Dempsey. "That's why I treasure the home movies of my parents' wedding in 1949.

"A few years ago I had those movies transferred to videotape, but that's not all. When my parents celebrated their 50th anniversary, they renewed their vows in front of their descendants. I videotaped the re-enactment and had it added to the 1949 footage. This blended tape preserves a history of love and commitment that will inspire generations to come."

HOME ★ MOVIES & TAPES

The Traveling Bong Show

The first year of marriage presents challenges for every couple such as where to spend Christmas. Since no one can be two places at once, Cricket and Jamie Newman decided to do the next best thing: appear in person in one place and appear on slides in the other.

"We decided we'd put together a slide show of our first year of marriage and send it to Nashville, where all of Jamie's family would be gathering," Cricket explains. "We began with our new apartment and closed with our first Christmas tree. For a special touch, we highlighted the red Christmas ball ornament with the word 'Jamie' in glitter. Since the slides were not self-explanatory, I audio-taped an accompanying poem. The signal for changing the slides was a resounding 'bong.'"

This enthusiastic young couple encountered a few challenges during the show's production. "For one thing," says Cricket, "the Christmas tree fell over. Luckily the historic red ball with Jamie's name in glitter survived the crash. We decided to include all of this in our show. Now, 22 years and two children later, I think it's time to transfer the slide show to DVD so our children can enjoy this *Family Original*,™ bongs and all."

Ideas!

- You and your family are stars in your own right, so produce your own home or garden tour. Let all family members participate. Children can narrate the tour of their rooms, playhouses or tree houses. One person can operate the camera; others can ask the questions; maybe someone can edit the film. The production will be its own story, and your tour is a great way to pass on knowledge and inspiration.

- Add new life to your old slides. Put them on a DVD and add commentary through voice-overs.

- Our voices are as unique as our fingerprints, so preserve yours by making a series of audiotapes of your memories. Future generations will be able to hear your story in your own words. You can record around "chapters" such as youth, career, early marriage, military, and parenting.

- Here's a unique gift idea for grandparents and relatives who live faraway: record your children's voices. They can be reading a poem or story, singing a favorite song, or talking about their day-to-day activities.

Tips for Videotaping

*From George O'Day of Capital Video
Columbia, South Carolina*

- Use a tripod to stabilize the camera.

- Avoid bright lights and windows behind the presenter.

- Position camera and subject away from distractions and interruptions.

- Presenter should wear clothing of medium shades of color.

- Use a clip-on microphone (available at Radio Shack for approximately $40).

- Position memorabilia to be discussed or shown nearby the presenter for easy referencing.

- Use the "standard play" recording mode for high-quality recording.

- Use high-grade videotape.

- Presenter should introduce himself or herself at the beginning.

- Presenter should have a prepared outline to follow or have someone asking questions to keep the story focused and on track.

- Presenter should be prepared to include details such as full names, specific dates and places.

- Presenter should wait several seconds before speaking. After the presenter is finished, allow the taping to continue for several seconds more before stopping.

Reel Life

It was "reel life" activity that took over the dining room. For Eric Lewis, though, it was merely an in-house video project for a reunion. He wanted to transfer 30 reels of 16mm movies onto videotape. Eric's project also served to preserve the fragile 16mm movies and thereby the stories, pictures and memories on these 1950s reels.

"I could get this done at a camera store," says Eric, "but with so many reels, I didn't want to pay that much. At about 10 cents a foot, it adds up in a hurry. Besides, I always love a project. I bought a video transfer box which you can use to transfer movies or slides to tape. My main advice to someone doing this is to buy high-quality videotape.

"I may eventually put my videos onto DVDs and add sound and captions. I'm really glad I didn't do that before the reunion, though. Half of my fun was listening to the reactions of everybody there. I had set up monitors in several places to show different videos simultaneously. One person said the only problem was deciding which one to watch."

If you have family movies, it's time to go "back to the future" by transferring them. Show them at your next family gathering or as entertainment for the grandchildren one evening. It's the best kind of reality show.

Try This...

List family members you know who took home movies. Contact them and plan a "Dinner and a Movie" evening. At your gathering, discuss creating a **Family Original** composite that will tell your family story.

_____
_____
_____
_____
_____
_____
_____
_____
_____
_____
_____
_____
_____
_____
_____
_____
_____
_____
_____
_____
_____

art

Starting with that first box of crayons, we learn to express ourselves through art. Those who become recognized for their talent, in all probability first exhibited their work on the family refrigerator. Some family members share their talent in original invitations and holiday cards as well as their drawings, paintings, pottery, and sculpture. Preserve these special *Family Originals*™ and the stories behind them.

Catherine W1

MY SKETCH BOOK

Pets and Palettes

"I have portraits of my cats, but not of my kids," says Karlyn Greenberg, who describes herself as always thinking and creating "outside the box." Her home and her life reflect her creative nature. One of her most interesting sets of paintings is, indeed, of her cats Pablo Picasso and Cat-Mandu (a play on Katmandu where the Siamese cat originated). Karlyn says, "One day I looked up on my kitchen counter, and Pablo was sitting there. It looked like the perfect subject for a painting, so I took a picture of the scene. I then painted that kitchen scene.

"Likewise," she continues, "I saw Mandu sitting on the limestone wall at our front door. It seemed just right to me, so I again took a picture and then painted it to immortalize Mandu on that wall. These pieces of artwork are my *Family Originals.*™"

Traveling Art

"When I was a college student studying in Florence, I was moved by the exquisite art, scenery and history all around me," says Catherine Lewis. "I was inspired to draw and paint as I sat in piazzas and toured museums. Instead of purchasing post cards to send to friends and family, I began making post card-sized paintings of my favorite places. These post cards chronicled my experiences as well as my studies."

Ideas!

Even though you may not be the artist in the family, you can express your creativity and thoughtfulness by adapting any of the following ideas for making **Family Originals.**

- Here's a fun gift idea for parents and grandparents to enjoy all year long. Turn children's art into a calendar. Let the artists choose the pictures. Any copy shop will take your 12 selections and print your calendar.

- Artwork and tableware. There are specialty stores and Web resources that will take original artwork and make it into fun and functional items such as coasters, plastic cups and plates. Take advantage of novelty items as a way to celebrate artistic talent in your family as you create these **Family Originals.**

- Make it personal. Turn original drawings into stationery, invitations, note cards, and holiday greeting cards. Most print shops can easily work with you on this project. It's a great way to share your artist's talents while communicating with friends and family.

- Put your original design on a t-shirt for a family celebration. A novelty store or custom t-shirt store can tell you how to do it. You can also go online and find resources under "creating t-shirts."

- Attention young parents. To encourage creativity in your child, select a place in your home where you display your child's artwork. Periodically change the exhibit. Also take a picture of the artist next to the exhibit before you change it.

- Create a family gallery on paper. Catalog pictures of art including paintings, sculpture, pottery, murals, and floor coverings. Tell the story behind each work, and include a photograph of the artist.

- You don't have to be an artist to appreciate art. What are your prized acquisitions from art shows, galleries or flea markets? Note your stories on cards and attach them to the pieces, if possible.

33.

Art

Art Award
to: Catherine Lewis
for having art displayed
for
Youth Art Month
Date: May, 1990

Bonnie Meine
Art Teacher

Gloria _____
Art Facil_____

No Starving Artists Allowed

"I always knew I was meant to follow a life in art, but my parents had another idea," says Caroline Graham. "They wanted my college major to lead to a job after graduation instead of the life of a 'starving artist.' Not to be outdone, I incorporated my artistic talents into my biology major. When I wrote my master's thesis on 'Phylogeny of the Ambrosiae,' I illustrated the entire paper with drawings." Caroline's thesis itself is a *Family Original.*™

Personal Touches

The influence of those who teach us lives on in many ways. "When I tried to purchase a particular painting at a professor's art show, I was outbid," remembers Christie Woodfin. "In the long run, though, I was not outdone. My professor offered to paint a work with me in mind. When he finished it, he explained, 'I painted this picture to symbolize you as my student. The peach blossoms represent a beautiful student struggling over school and the decisions you need to make in life; there is a cloud over the sun, but the sun keeps shining through, and the trees continue to bloom.'

"In each portrait or still life I paint now," Christie continues, "I always include a meaningful item that tells a story."

Sidney Gauthreaux, a renowned ornithologist, loves to draw and paint. He shares his expertise and talent in an annual holiday card he and Carroll send. These cards have become collectors' items, and recipients look forward to receiving a new one each year. Some have framed theirs for prominent display.

Try This...

Who are the artists in your family? List them here. Describe their artwork, and the inspiration behind it. You have now begun researching your **Family Original** History of Art.

_____
_____
_____
_____
_____
_____
_____
_____
_____
_____
_____
_____
_____
_____
_____
_____
_____
_____

Empty Nest and Full Palette

When Susalee Lamb's children went off to college, she enrolled in a weekly art class. Within three months, she had painted this wonderful portrait of her brother's beloved dog. She gave it to her brother for Christmas and, since then, has painted other meaningful portraits for family members. As a gift to the artist, family members are compiling a catalog of Susalee's works. This catalog and her portraits are special *Family Originals.*™

Textiles & Needlework

A Stitch in Time for All Time

Needlework is a metaphor for life with its infinite texture, color, pattern, and design. These pieces of the family story can surface on a table, sofa, floor, wall, bed, and even our very person. They enhance major events such as baptisms, holidays and weddings. They also add function and form to beauty and reflect countless hours of love, commitment and creativity that can be passed on from generation to generation.

Ideas!

- Loving hands produce lasting works. Create a **Family Original** catalog with photographs of handwork that has been embroidered, crocheted, knitted, smocked, hemstitched, and cross-stitched. Include information about the artist, the inspiration for the handwork, and all the places each work of art has traveled. Add stories you've heard about the role these pieces have played in family life.

- Quick Tip. From smocked dresses to knitted sweaters, handwork is often wearable art. For those pieces, take a photograph to record the work, the artist and the model. Don't forget to add pertinent facts on the back of your photos, and include them in your **Family Original** catalog.

- Turn an heirloom quilt into a decorative wall hanging or display it on a quilt stand. To preserve its history, take a picture and note its story on a card. The picture and story can go in your **Family Original** catalog.

- If you have a hand-made rag rug or hooked rug, or even an oriental rug you inherited, include the story and a photograph in your **Family Original** catalog.

- Stitches on the wall: Frame special pieces of needlework from cross stitch to needlepoint. On the back, tell their story.

- Add a personal dimension to your holiday tables by using linens that tell a story. Keep your camera loaded. On the back of each picture from the celebration, note the needlework as well as the people.

Angels with Her

People long for ways to demonstrate love for someone who is sick, to remember someone who is moving away, or to recognize an achievement or important occasion in a special person's life. A friendship quilt is one way to do that.

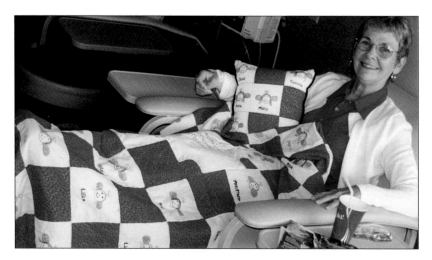

One of the most thoughtful examples of this type love gift is the quilt created for Jackie Brittingham by friends and family. "I never go to chemotherapy without it," Jackie says, "and every time I go, this quilt not only ministers to me, but to someone else, both nurses and patients."

To create the quilt, a group of special people gathered, and each one signed an angel square. In the large square in the center are these words: "Angels Are Praying for You." What an extraordinary expression of love and support.

The Handwriting on the Cloth

A well-known motivational speaker tells the story of growing up on a college campus where her parents opened their home to visiting scholars, dignitaries and interesting guests. Her mother asked each dinner guest to sign the white tablecloth. Before laundering the cloth, her mother embroidered over each new signature. Now this treasure with many famous autographs captures a special chapter in the history of campus life.

Textiles & Needlework

The relationship between a hunter and his Lab can be honored in needlework. For a special touch, attach information on the back about the hunter and dog, as well as the artist.

The year Jere Eggleston retired, he turned a hobby into an avocation and made it official in a marketing brochure. For Christmas that year, a family member created a *Family Original.*™  Armed with the brochure, she hired someone in a needlework shop to graph the design. Then she completed a cross stitch of the design. The gift became a true family project when another family member framed the needlework in a do-it-yourself framing shop. The look on Jere's face that Christmas when he opened the gift is the best part of the story.

If you like to cross stitch, you can make a *Family Original*™ from a meaningful document. Be sure to chronicle the story on the back of the frame.

Memory Quilt

"I was so touched when I was presented this extraordinary quilt," says Cora Sue Mach. "It was a thank-you gift for my volunteer service as president of the Crohn's & Colitis Foundation of America."

This handmade quilt displays pictures of Cora Sue at CCFA functions and fund raisers. With this unique treasure, Cora Sue doubly enjoys "warm and touching" memories of her year as president and her time with the volunteers who worked with her.

Patchwork of Love

Stephanie Jamison has created a patchwork of talent, history and love not just once but twice. She has one more creation to go before she can holster that needle and put down her sewing machine. You see, Stephanie has made a graduation quilt for two of her three daughters as a tangible and touching bridge between home and college.

These priceless quilts reflect family and history in featured photographs. They also reflect family and history in featured memorabilia such as a grandmother's jewelry, a grandfather's military buttons and pins from his World War II collection, antique lace and decorative trim from fashionable clothing of yesteryear.

Trinkets in the attic and clutter in drawers can lead to original needlework and cherished gifts from the heart to share with those we love.

Ideas!

- Turn a tablecloth into history. Let friends and relatives sign a white cloth, and then embroider the signatures. You can include names, dates and events.

- Have a child sign a white linen napkin each year and embroider over the signature. This child will have a set of 12 when high school graduation comes around.

- Mark the date. A special way to create an heirloom christening gown is to embroider on the hem the name and baptismal date of every baby who wears it. Over the years the gown will become a recorded history of faith and family.

- Here's a great gift idea. Put together a celebration quilt. Start by giving friends or relatives squares for writing their message to the recipient. Be sure to use permanent ink. If you choose, you can embroider messages as well. You don't have to assemble the quilt yourself. You can consult resources in the phone book or on the Web. Start by looking under "quilts." Present the quilt as a toast to a bride and groom, as a gift to a graduate, or as a going-away gift from friends and neighbors.

- Don't forget the textiles you've acquired from friends, travels and even flea markets. They tell stories, too. Preserve them in your **Family Original** catalog.

Textiles & Needlework

The Million Dollar Stocking

"I am as proud of that Christmas stocking as I am my PHD," proclaims Dr. Patty Mahlstedt. "The inspiration was my husband's grandmother, who had needlepointed stockings for our three children. When I became a grandmother for the first time, I decided to continue that tradition. Besides, I had done lots of 'basket weave' needlepoint projects and loved doing them.

"The project, however, took on a life of its own. In two months' time, I had not only made a stocking; I had made what our family now calls a 'Million Dollar Stocking.' When I purchased the painted canvas, the saleslady asked me if I wanted her 'to make a stitch guide and pull the threads for it.' Of course I said 'yes' without realizing it meant using all sorts of fancy stitches and numerous expensive threads. That stitch guide was Greek to me. It did not involve any of the basic stitching that I knew how to do. Consequently, I had to go to needlepoint class. By the time I finished the stocking, I had taken classes in two different shops, paid for extra accessories, and purchased several instruction books.

"However, when I completed the 'Million Dollar Stocking,' all the extra costs became secondary to the hours of love and devotion I had poured into that project. I treasure the time I spent making the stocking and my family enjoys telling the story. I know my grandson will treasure my creation when he grows older."

Handmade Christmas stockings are priceless holiday decorations in many homes. Is there a story behind the stockings hanging on your mantle?

Generation to Generation

The baptismal gown that Betsy Moore is wearing has been worn by every baby in her family for four generations. This *Family Original*™ tells a story of faith and family ties which connect generations. It is being preserved for future infant baptisms.

It's never too late to begin your own tradition. Upon the arrival of a first grandchild, you could make or purchase the baptismal dress to be used and preserved for generations to come.

Ideas!

- Here's a clever way to recycle old t-shirts: turn them into a quilt. The squares are the decorative graphics from the t-shirts. The t-shirts may have come from faraway places, college parties, clubs and organizations, competitions, rock concerts, causes, vacations, or family reunions. They make wonderful birthday, graduation and anniversary gifts. Keep in mind you do not have to make the quilt yourself. Consult the phone book or the Web for resources.

- "Pillow Talk". Turn those t-shirts into pillows instead of quilts.

- Make pillows from other "raw materials" such as military insignia, scout badges and antique family lace.

Packaged Diehl

In the process of moving, Ottie Lee Baker found a box of pre-cut fabric pieces for a quilt she had intended to make. Instead of feeling guilty or throwing the pieces away, Ottie Lee gave them to her granddaughter Gwen Diehl. Realizing the potential, Gwen hired a quilter to complete the project. Wrapped in the now-finished quilt are Ottie Lee and her great grandson Justin. Gwen likes to think of this picture as a "Packaged Diehl."

The Continuous Thread

Jill and Togar White were unable to attend the baptism of their first grand-child, so Jill did the next-best thing. She sent the baptismal gown for her grand-daughter Campbell. But this was no ordinary baptismal gown. Instead, it was a dress Jill had made from her wedding dress.

Always one to be prepared, Jill saved enough material from her wedding dress to make a baptismal suit for a grandson, just in case there is one.

★ NEWSPAPER CLIPPINGS ★

Programs and Bulletins

In a meeting of minds, the e-world links up with its creative comrades to raise Atlanta's cultural profile — and the new businesses' ability to convince young, skilled workers that this city is the place to be

THE (INTER)FACE OF ARTS AND TECHNOLOGY

MARC ADLER: Founder of Macquarium Intelligent Communications

JOHN BACON: President and CEO of Iterated Systems

By Tom Sabulis
tsabulis@ajc.com

IT'S a meeting of palette and pixel.

Newspaper clippings often make *Family Originals*™ in themselves. If a family member has been featured in a magazine or newspaper, frame the article for a special gift.

The Times and the Timeless

"Have you ever looked for something, only to find something else much better? That's what happened to me when I started looking for one particular newspaper column my father had written," says Lucie Eggleston. "I ended up reading every single column—all 490 of them. My father had died 23 years before, and, through the re-discovery of his columns, I had him with me again…talking to me, helping me see things in a different perspective, gently guiding me. In the process, I realized a book of these columns was a gift I could give my entire family, and that's what I did in 1993. At the beginning of the collection, I wrote:

The collection gives all of us who knew and loved Da the special blessing of rereading his "Thoughts," of hearing once again his voice, and of knowing in a way his values, his faith and his spirit.

As you read his words, I feel sure you'll have the same multi-faceted response I did. You'll laugh out loud… you'll be amazed at his extensive knowledge which ranges from "the history of sausage" to stories of pivotal personalities and events in the unfolding of human history. You'll be moved by the depth of his patriotism, his devotion to family, his love of humanity, and his abiding faith."

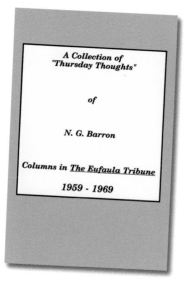

A Collection of
"Thursday Thoughts"

of

N. G. Barron

Columns in *The Eufaula Tribune*

1959 - 1969

Ideas!

- Here's a quick and easy way to tackle, tame and distribute paper memorabilia. Think INSIDE the box. Collect a loved one's birthday cards, report cards, certificates, newspaper clippings, programs, and simply put them in a box. Save the boxed memories for a time when the family is together. Then start thinking OUTSIDE the box. Give everyone the appropriate memory box and ask each person to select an item for impromptu storytelling.

- If your family has a Web page, it's the perfect place to organize and showcase your paper history. Include appropriate photographs with your media accounts.

- Découpage is making a comeback, and it's an ideal way to preserve printed items. If craft projects appeal to you, create a "paper trail" of memories in items ranging from place mats to planters and trash cans to toy chests.

- Newspaper clippings, programs, and bulletins add interest and variety to the family photo album.

- What original manuscripts are residing in your boxes, closets or bookshelves? Consider duplicating and binding them as a gift for other family members.

- Looking for a clever party invitation? With the help of a good print shop, you can use newspaper clippings to create a custom-made invitation to a current event.

★ NEWSPAPER CLIPPINGS ★

Programs and Bulletins

EUFAULA HI-TIMES

VOLUME XI

NUMBER 6

THE EUFAULA HI-TIMES, Tuesday, May 24, 1960

EUFAULA HIGH SCHOOL SENIOR CLASS OF 1960

First row, left to right: Beryl Doughtie, Glenda Bell, Suzan Motley, Gatra ... ...burn Sewell, Jean Dismukes, Sandra Johnson, Jewel Green, Karla ... ... Bobbie Segars, Mary Hicks, Melba Jean Parker, ... Donald Pollock, Pete Head, Sonn... ...th Clenny, ... Gle...

Dallas Country Day School May Festival 1951

Skipper Horn age 8½

Staff Photograph by Jeff Zehr

Andy Hamilton takes Annabell on her daily stroll on a quiet Tuesday afternoon near his home on Forest Drive.

The Andy Barron Times

VOLUME 1, ISSUE 1   May 1998

Barron changes jobs twice in 1998

CHAPEL HILL, NC –Andrew Barron's push to find a new line of work took a sudden and happy turn as he was hired by the University of North Carolina.

'I had my sights set on Chapel Hill from the start of my job search.' - Andy Barron

Andy Barron shared good news in this entertaining, informative *Family Original.™* His inspiration was three-fold: a new house, a new job and a supportive family he wanted to thank. Since all the members of Andy's immediate family participated in these major decisions, he featured their roles, quotes and all. Grandparents, aunts, uncles, and cousins received the news and enjoyed every single sentence.

Your life is always newsworthy to the people you love. Put the major events of your life on the front page of your very own publication.

Clippings from Orene's Garden
A Southern Gardener's Year
Orene Horton

Garden Clippings

Gardening connects us to the earth and to each other. It is also a metaphor for life's cycles with its seasons, growth, beauty, color, and variety. Orene Horton, a lifelong gardener and gifted teacher, shared her expertise in a weekly column in *The State* newspaper. For years, she instructed and inspired people who never even met her, even in the midst of her courageous battle with breast cancer. Her husband Tate has collected her columns in a beautifully published book entitled *Clippings from Orene's Garden*. Through this living memorial, Tate has ensured Orene will continue to teach future generations.

Try This...

If you have saved newspaper clippings, programs and bulletins, now is the time to revisit them. As you go through the piles, list various ways to sort these priceless items (by family member, activity or date). You have now started your own **Family Original** Special Edition.

_____
_____
_____
_____
_____
_____
_____
_____
_____
_____

Lead Story

"My father-in-law began the day with a cup of coffee and *The Wall Street Journal*," remembers Frank Brown. "It occurred to me there ought to be a way to connect his morning ritual and his 80th birthday. We came up with the idea of telling his life story in the format of the *Journal*.

"I enlisted some professional help. For one thing, I used a writer who had a knack for mimicking style. I supplied the facts, and he added the flair. Then I took that copy to a professional printer. Keep in mind I did this in the early 80s, but you could probably do this today with your computer.

"My father-in-law got a big kick out of it, but the truth is, I believe we had the most fun of all. The framed tribute hangs in our home today, so his life story continues to interact with ours."

Photo opportunity ...

Maybe you stash them in a drawer. Maybe you hide them in a closet. Maybe they're collecting dust under the bed or in the attic.

We're talking pictures. Family treasures. Precious memories.

But after the fun of taking photographs, then seeing them developed, it's a lot easier to hide them than to take the time to get them identified, dated and organized in some sort of album.

To the rescue comes Lucy Lewis, at right, who leads "Creative Memories" workshops. She teaches regular folks who are not professional photographers how to store photographs.

Lewis became interested in the business several years ago when she was looking for a good way to preserve her daughter's travel pictures. She ran into a woman selling Creative Memories supplies, dropped a bundle, then stopped to think.

"That was the easiest sale that lady ever had," Lewis says. "I went back, asked her about her business and took a class."

Before long, Lewis was offering seminars, too. "First I tell people that our products are safe for their pictures," Lewis says. "The paper is acid-free. Beyond that, everyone wants the photos to be meaningful. That means writing who, what, when and where on the back. You think you'll remember — but you know how fast that goes.

"I saw one photo ID that said 'Me.' 'Me' is not enough."

— CLAUDIA FELDMAN

Betty Tichich / Chronicle

Journals, Letters & e-mail

首都师范大学外国语学院
(阜外白堆子甲 23 号)

Capital Normal University
College of Foreign Languages
Beijing China
Postcode 100037

Mrs. Marion H. Hamilton
400 Da Vega Dr. Box 14
Lexington, SC 29073
USA

航　空
PAR AVION

29071/0014

Postscripts

We long to connect with those we love who themselves are experiencing sorrow. One person discovered a way to do this. When his wife was in the final stages of a terminal illness, he wrote to each person in her address book and made a request. He asked each one to write his wife a letter "and say everything to her you were planning to say to me about her after her death."

The response was overwhelming. Her final days were flooded with expressions of love and meaning from people whose lives she had deeply touched and influenced. It also gave those close to her a way to communicate their love and support. These tributes to her wonderful life created a beautiful closing chapter.

Written words are priceless personal documents, but don't overlook the power of the human voice. As one person said after reading letters written by his grandfather who died before he was born: "I love reading his words, but I can't hear his voice." Consider recording select journal entries and letters, thus creating your own "book-on-tape" for future generations.

Ideas!

CAUTION!

Journals and letters are tricky.

You never want to invade another person's privacy, but when the entries seem "safe" for sharing, the message is powerful.

- Start a tradition. On your children's birthdays, write an annual letter. You can mention things you enjoy and admire about your children now as well as your hopes and aspirations for them later. Include a note or two about what is going on in their lives as well as in the world at their particular age. This annual letter of love and history can lead to a collection to present to each child at a later milestone in life.

- Write a letter to your children at any significant time in their lives such as a baptism, graduation or wedding day. Letters describing these momentous occasions are a wonderful way to chronicle family life.

- Forget keeping a daily journal. Instead, when given the opportunity, focus on a special chapter in your life such as "Studying Abroad," "My Time in Alaska," "Student Teaching," "Special Assignments," "Short-term Missionary," and "Championship Seasons." You can enhance the journals with corresponding photographs.

- Play the numbers game with your journal entries. For a personal anniversary or birthday gift, select journal entries about the person you are honoring. Be sure to date the excerpts. Choose the number of entries that corresponds to the anniversary or birthday being celebrated, like 15 selections for a 15th anniversary or birthday.

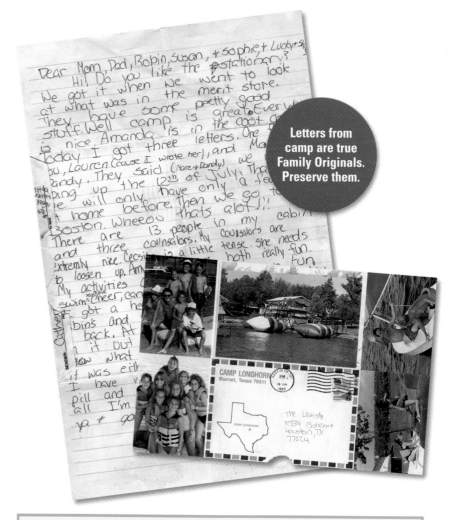

Letters from camp are true Family Originals. Preserve them.

Colors for Granny

To honor Mabel Paulus at age 95, every member of her family wrote her a letter. The great grandchildren who were too young to write drew pictures. Each person focused on something special about their relationship with Mabel. Since she and her son-in-law love new words and crossword puzzles, his letter teased Mabel with its challenging vocabulary. The "letter" from Mabel's youngest descendant was a picture in fuchsia and teal, two of Mabel's favorite colors. The young artist told her mother, "These are colors God made for Granny."

Mabel's daughter collected the letters in an album whose cover also told Mabel's story. The cover incorporated fabric, buttons and lace from vintage garments in Mabel's closet. This album truly is a *Family Original!*™

Journals, Letters & e-mail

View toward Greve - eve of the clearest night — Tuscany
after dark we could
see lights on most distant hills almost to Florence
Millions of tiny fireflies looks like Christmas twinkle lights

Caroline Graham teaches art and leads painting excursions in the U.S., Europe and Mexico. When she travels, she keeps a book of sketches and paintings. She includes her thoughts and specific information about people and vistas. Sometimes she goes back to paint larger pieces using the sketchbook renditions.

"This approach somehow evolved," says Caroline. "It has become so meaningful and useful to me, I now teach it to my students. It's a wonderful way to chronicle my travel experiences while I experiment in style and form."

Technology with a Touch

It's easy to assume e-mails are not collectors' items, but just the opposite can be true. In fact, they inspired a special gift from one daughter to her mother. The Christmas after her first child was born, Meg Christian gave her mother, Eleanor Barron, a collection of all the e-mails Eleanor had written to Meg during the preceding year, a very significant year. "Dear Pooh, A Collection of E-mails from Mother to Daughter" was arranged in four categories: Engagement, Wedding, Pregnancy, and Birth. Within each category, Meg presented the e-mails chronologically.

"It is one of my most treasured possessions," says Eleanor. "Every time I read those e-mails, I'm reminded of the incredible year I became a mother-in-law and grandmother. Sadly, it was also the year of September 11."

Run, Mommy, Run!

Journals, like the people who keep them, come in all types and sizes. There are travel journals, prayer journals, baby journals, and gardening journals. Lynlee Linke even keeps an exercise journal. A marathon runner, Lynlee comes from an athletic family and chronicles the importance of training and exercise in her life.

She began running for health and stress relief. Once she delivered her twin daughters, she also wanted to lose weight. To add a social element to her exercise routine, she started running with a neighbor. Then her husband joined the cause. He has even run several 5K races.

Now a family affair, Lynlee pushes her twins in the double running stroller. If she slows down to a walk, the twins chime in together, "Run, Mommy, Run!" That has become the universal cry in the family when someone needs to hurry up.

Along with her journal, Lynlee has an album that includes journal excerpts, corresponding photographs, entry numbers from her races, and newspaper accounts of the marathons. These materials would also work well in a collage.

Ideas!

- If you send an annual holiday letter, you are a family historian. Collect your letters from years past, and duplicate the collection for family members. Add corresponding pictures if you have them. This special gift of personal history will also show you how family life has changed over the years.

- Here's a thoughtful, easy way to unload excess memorabilia. Simply "Return to Sender." Think of the pleasure you'll give the recipients when they open an envelope and encounter moments and memories from their past. On occasion, enclose a meaningful photograph.

- Don't forget the power of the Web. Personal Web pages are created every day to foster communication for various reasons: congratulatory messages, updates on illnesses, reunion planning. This dynamic medium simultaneously records personal history in the making. If you have never created a Web page and want additional information, just type "how to make a Web page" into any search engine for a list of resources. There are also books on the subject.

- Here's an easy tip for new parents. Use calendar pages to note special events as they happen. Chronicle visitors, gifts, outings and milestones as they happen to create a day-to-day journal of those first important months.

Chain Letter, Family Style

Virginia Burrows Murray comes from a large family that "refuses to break the chain." This chain started in the 1920s when Virginia's father, the oldest of eight children, wrote a letter and sent it to the next in line. This one, in turn, added a letter about his family and sent the two letters to sibling #3. The process continued through the eighth sibling. Then he sent the entire collection back to the eldest, who had started the process.

The oldest child then removed the letter he had first written, wrote a new one, and mailed the new one along with the seven others. He also saved all his own letters once they had made the rounds. Imagine having your own family's history so completely recorded in letters.

The next generation has continued the chain. The cousins still route family news through this collection they have named "The Bird," because the news "flies from nest to nest."

Would this letter-writing process be a great way for your family to stay in touch as well as archive your family history? Such a collection *is* a **Family Original**.™

Try This...

Think of letters, journals and personal e-mails you have saved. List those that come to mind. There is a reason you have saved each one. Note those reasons. Then think of people who would enjoy reading excerpts and your corresponding reflections. You are well on your way to creating a **Family Original** collection.

_____
_____
_____
_____
_____
_____
_____
_____
_____
_____
_____
_____
_____
_____
_____
_____
_____
_____
_____
_____
_____
_____
_____
_____
_____
_____

Decorative Objects & Décor

Object Lessons

Objects tell powerful stories. Just think of

the popularity of television shows such as

"Antiques Roadshow." Your own objects link

you to people, places and experiences.

Maybe it's your grandmother's china you get

out every Thanksgiving or the prized piece of

pottery you nursed all the way home from a

faraway place. Treat the stories with the

same care you give the objects themselves.

When Bob Eggleston looks at his butterfly collection, he thinks about childhood summer days on Edisto Island, running barefoot with a butterfly net in his hand. The unique collection is extraordinary because of the number of species displayed, but it is particularly special because Bob's father crafted the shadowbox to house this collection.

Ideas!

- Go on a guided tour of any historic home and listen to the docents describe the furnishings. Your furnishings tell stories, too. What are your favorite pieces, and what stories do they tell? Photograph those special objects, and tell their stories in a family catalog. The catalog is a great gift for family members.

- Here's a fun way to light up your history. Take a meaningful object such as an antique tea pot or an old watering can and turn it into a lamp.

- The stories of your meaningful objects need to stay with them. One way to guarantee that happens is to video your own "docu-memory." Have family members talk about their favorite objects and the stories behind them. The camera operator needs to pan the object as well as the storyteller. You will have a **Family Original** for the silver screen, history books and your insurance company.

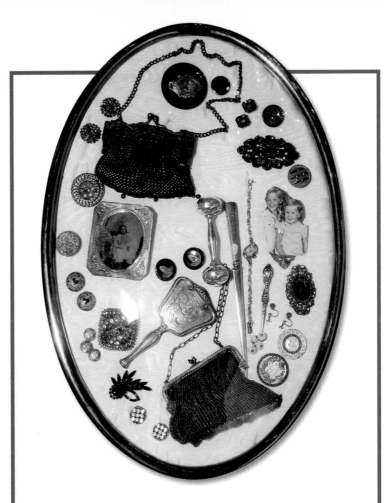

What do you do with a myriad of trinkets? Jerri Shaw Ashbeck created a wedding gift with her grandmother's evening purses and costume jewelry, vintage buttons from heirloom dresses, silver baby rattle, and old family pictures. Jerri's nephew and his bride now have the treasured *Family Original.*™

Traveling Salesmen and Miniature Furniture

Diane Strong can make a very interesting catalog of her collection of miniatures which are museum quality. In the 18th and 19th centuries, furniture makers had limited ways of promoting their craft. To give prospective buyers an example of their craftsmanship, they made exquisite miniature furniture models for salesmen to show. Today these rare miniatures are greatly prized, but the greater value for Diane is the personal story behind the collection she inherited from her grandmother.

Decorative Objects & Décor

Death by Pitchfork and Flo Blue Plates

In the kitchen hutch in a house in Alabama is a set of Flo Blue plates. If those plates could talk, they would tell you this story.

In the 1920s in Abingdon, Virginia, Mr. John Litton, Sheriff of Washington County, got into an argument with his neighbor because the neighbor's livestock repeatedly crossed the property line and uprooted his garden. When the argument started, John Litton was holding a pitchfork. In the heat of the moment, he hit his neighbor, unwittingly dealing a fatal blow.

John Litton had been reared by his widowed aunt, Clemmie Hawthorne, who appealed to Judge F. B. Hutton to defend her nephew. Judge Hutton agreed to take the case *pro bono*.

That Christmas Eve there was a timid knock at the Judge's door. Aunt Clemmie stood there with six blue plates. "I remember one night you came to my house to help my boy John with his trial, and you mentioned these were pretty plates. I want you to have them."

In the seven decades since that Christmas Eve, those plates have traveled with the Judge's daughter from Virginia to Alabama by way of Georgia and South Carolina. One day those plates will travel to another house, and their story needs to go with them.

Artistic License and Portrait Restoration

When Christine Theriot was a young girl, her mother commissioned John Clay Parker, a well-known Louisiana artist, to paint Christine's portrait. This portrait then hung in a prominent place in the Theriot home in New Orleans. One day Christine's brother climbed onto an antique chair and drew a moustache on this work of art. With the exception of Christine's brother, everyone was upset. No one knew, however, how to eliminate the moustache, and the portrait continued to hang in its prominent place. For her part, Christine's solution was to retaliate with a moustache on her brother's portrait. Her parents intervened and, therefore, justice was never served.

One day Christine's cousin Ruth Crull came to visit. She happened to be a graduate student in research chemistry. She took it upon herself to restore the portrait. She climbed on a chair and got rid of the moustache. Never mind the need for chemistry and chemicals. She used a plain gum eraser to remove the pencil marks. It took visiting cousin Ruth to restore not only the portrait but Christine's dignity as well.

The moustache lives on, however, in the telling and re-telling of this story.

Neck and Neck

Jewelry almost always tells a story. This azure necklace spans four generations and is now worn proudly by the great grand-daughter of its original owner, Edna Robbins Herrick. Edna's daughter and granddaughter kept the necklace in a jewelry box for years. Then it made its way back into style and into the great granddaughter's hands. Its story is one reason she enjoys wearing this *Family Original*™.

Do you have old and interesting pieces of jewelry in your family? Styles may skip a generation, but stories about family heirlooms are forever.

"I Never Outgrew My First Pair of Shoes"

"Those are my baby shoes." says Christie Woodfin proudly as she points to the decorative bookends in her living room. "My mother had the shoes bronzed when I was little, and I had them made into bookends. With these in my living room, I'll never outgrow my love of books or my first pair of shoes."

What objects do you have from other chapters in your life, and how can you adapt them for your current lifestyle?

Decorative Objects & Décor

The Wedding Gift

Alice Pearce needlepointed this exquisite bellpull as a wedding gift for her cousin, and one day it will become an heirloom. Its story needs to be recorded now to accompany this labor of love as it moves through time and generations.

Think about your list of wedding gifts as an historical document. This list is a starting place for cataloging your decorative objects.

The Baptismal Gift

This proud grandfather wanted a small but sentimental way to remember his granddaughter Susan on the occasion of her infant baptism. As he had collected silver dollars over the years, he chose one of his oldest coins as his gift to her.

When his granddaughter became a young lady, she decided to have the silver dollar made into a necklace. Not only does this wonderful piece of jewelry elicit compliments, but it also elicits questions which allow Susan to tell her family story.

Gone with the Wind and Back to the Future

This lamp was originally an oil lamp. During the Civil War, as the northern army entered Mississippi, Irene Nunnery's family buried this brass lamp on the plantation "to protect it from the Yankees." Today this interesting antique with its personal history is in the home of Irene's daughter.

Planned Giving

"Start early to collect special gifts for graduates," advises Kathy Arnold. She should know. During the four years her daughter was in high school, Kathy searched for and collected antique linen handkerchiefs. "My goal was to find linens that were monogrammed with the corresponding initials of Elizabeth's friends." Upon graduation those friends were amazed and touched by the sincerity, care and time that had gone into the purchasing of these personal gifts. Kathy was equally touched by their gratitude.

Try This...

Think about special gifts you've received through the years. List them here. Note their meaning for you. You have just completed the first step in your collection of "object lessons."

_____
_____
_____
_____
_____
_____
_____
_____
_____
_____
_____
_____
_____
_____
_____
_____
_____
_____
_____
_____
_____
_____
_____

Advice, Wisdom & Family Lore

The richest resource of all is the experience housed in the human heart. An easy way to tap this resource is to ask members of your family about their life experiences. Then sit back and enjoy what follows.

It Can be Done.

Ann Marie McNamara videotapes her mother Margaret Mathis telling the extraordinary stories of her childhood growing up in Paris in the 1920s. Ann is using a book of questions she found in a bookstore.

A Bicycle Built for Two

Do you believe in love at first sight? Brad Beutel certainly does. The first time he saw his future wife, he was looking out of a bus window, and she was standing on the sidewalk. He knew he had to ask her out. When he called her to ask her for a date, the 15-year-old Pam replied, "I am not allowed to 'car-date' until I turn 16."

Brad was not discouraged. He arrived at her house one afternoon on a rented bicycle built for two to take her out for ice cream. Pam's parents were stunned at the ingenious way Brad bent their rule. A relative was so impressed with Brad's creative tenacity that she recounted this story as her toast at their rehearsal party seven years later.

Lessons of a Lifetime

Interview family members to hear their "lessons of a lifetime." Turn this wisdom into a Family Anthology of Advice. On individual pages, include the advice, the story that validated the advice, and the family member's name and picture. This would be a fabulous gift to duplicate and give to family members.

Lessons of a Lifetime

Advice

_____
_____
_____
_____
_____

Story that validated the advice

_____
_____
_____
_____
_____
_____

Family member's name and picture

_____

Advice, Wisdom & Family Lore

The Contest

"Grandma never shows partiality," declares Richard Barron. "There have certainly been times we tried to ask her to pick sides in an argument, but she never gave in. One time, while visiting her, my sister Meg and I were drawing pictures. I was 6 and Meg was 4. Although you could attribute my ability to age and two years' more practice, there was no disputing my superior coloring and drawing ability. So, while drawing, I commented to Meg that my art was better than hers. Meg, not backing down, insisted that hers was better. We needed a judge.

"We took our pieces to Grandma, who simply called it a tie. She said they were both wonderful, and then she sent us back to draw a horse. We did and then came back with our best renditions of a stallion. Still, we were tied. I tried pointing out how my drawing had better detail and was anatomically correct. It didn't matter. We were still tied. The same thing happened with the drawing of a house.

"Finally, I went to the kitchen with Meg, where I told her we would each make one more drawing. But this time, I would take BOTH pictures to Grandma, claiming both as my own. Grandma fell for the trap. When pushed for an answer, she said, 'I do believe I like this one a little better,' holding MY picture. When Meg got upset, Grandma consoled her and immediately picked one of her drawings as better than another one of mine, bringing us back into a tie. Meg insists that such a sinister plan could have only been mine and denies any part of coming up with the idea.

"A cute story it is, but it is also quite indicative of Grandma's unfailing and equal love she feels for all of us. She has never once done anything to make any of us feel anything but special—not an easy task when you have eight grandchildren all pulling for your attention. A fine example she set."

Writing Tips

1. **The essence of our lives is remembered in moments.** Record them. Think of specific incidents and quotes. Start at the beginning of the story and imagine you are telling it to someone else. "When I was 6 years old, my Aunt Myrtle came to visit." You can "tell it on paper," or tell it into a recorder and transcribe it later.

2. **Use concrete details.**
   • "Miss Rossie Andrews, my third-grade piano teacher" not "My music teacher."
   • "Christmas 2000" not "One Christmas."
   • "My first day waiting tables" not "My part-time job."
   • "When we toured the Capitol Building" not "While I was on vacation."

3. **Choose your favorite medium.** If you like to have a pen in your hand, record your stories in your own handwriting. If you prefer the computer, use it.

4. **Brainstorm a list of incidents to record.** Here are some from John Bacon, whose daughter asked him to record stories of his childhood.
   • Christmas Tree Forts • Charlie Greengrass and the Science Project
   • Show and Tell with the Table Saw • Model T with Missing Parts

By Way of Introduction

If you're planning a baby shower, consider involving the guests in creating a *Family Original.*™ Janet Roberson Sumner gave guests the following template and then put the completed pages in an album. At the shower, she took a picture of each guest for the collection.

You can adapt this idea for a bride, a graduate or a retiree.

Your family

My name is

I am your

What I enjoy most about your mother is

What I enjoy most about your father is

I want you to know this about me

The first thing I want to tell you is

Ideas!

- Here's a quick and colorful way to "plant" a family tree. Tape the stories of how couples met, or collect those stories in an album and include the wedding announcement and the wedding picture.

- Everybody has a favorite book, so why don't you interview members of every generation about their favorite books? In the process, you will create a recommended reading list, another **Family Original**. Some reading lists may surprise you and even motivate you to reread a favorite book. You could also make your own book-on-tape for children and grandchildren to play in the car on family trips.

- Here's a novel idea for a family gathering. Ask family members to bring favorite poems and literary passages. Then tape each person reading selections. Duplicate the tape for everyone to enjoy, especially on long trips.

- Most of us struggle to find the perfect gift for loved ones. Here's an idea: give your favorite books and write in each an inscription about why you love the book.

- Host a "Family Tell-a-thon." Let family members put topics for stories in a hat ("vacations," "holidays," "pets"). Once everyone has drawn a topic, record the stories.

Knight on a White Horse

Who says that chivalry is dead? Laurie Towns knows better. When she and her future husband, Bo, were counselors at camp, Bo arranged a concert for all the campers—or so he said. Once the 400 campers were assembled, Bo revealed the real purpose for the gathering. Dressed as a knight in shining armor, he rode into the amphitheater on the back of a white horse. A stunned Laurie froze as Bo walked on stage. Then he knelt at her feet.

"Will you marry me?" he asked. For a moment Laurie remained speechless, but not the campers. All 400 took over. "Say yes!" they screamed. When Laurie caught her breath and tearfully nodded her acceptance, Bo led her off the stage, lifted her atop the white horse, and they rode off into the sunset. The only downside to this family story is the standard Bo set for other suitors.

Try This...

Make a list of your favorite people. Think of one story about the first person on your list and jot it down. Now go to the next person. You will soon have a collection of meaningful stories.

_____
_____
_____
_____
_____
_____
_____
_____
_____
_____
_____
_____
_____
_____
_____
_____
_____
_____
_____
_____
_____
_____
_____

Graduations

FOURTH OF JULY

Pets

MILITARY

Anniversaries & Weddings

BIRTHDAYS

Sports

Easter

Cars

REUNIONS

Mother's Day & Father's Day

Vacations Houses

THANKSGIVING

Christmas

COSTUMES Faith

The best way to "get your hands around" all those memories is to choose a theme. Then sort all the memorabilia relating to that theme and watch your story emerge.

BiRTHdAYS

MAY 1957

You Take the Cake

Throughout your life, your birthday is the one day that's uniquely yours. The cake has your name on it and so do the gifts. When you blow out the candles, you can wish for anything you want. Therefore, when loved ones look for a time to honor you, they need look no further than your birthday...especially if it's classified as "a *big* one." Likewise, you can draw from countless memories to create *Family Originals*™ for every member of your family. Adult birthday parties let us all celebrate the child in us and the precious gift of life itself. Some children's birthday celebrations touch the timeless such as dress-up parties and backyard camp-outs. Other party themes reflect the times, such as Spiderman, Barbie, The Lone Ranger, and Dick Tracy. To record these memories, therefore, is to record history.

BIRTHDAYS

1. Looking for an easy way to record your family's story while you're living it?
Start with the next birthday in your family. Collect photographs and memories of that occasion. Be sure to record pertinent information on the back of each photo with a pen available at scrapbooking and art supply stores.

Repeat this activity for the next person's birthday. Keep the process going for each birthday; at the end of the year, you can quickly put together a collage of photos of birthdays during that year. You can entitle it "A Year in the Life of Our Family."

Start this easy activity now. As the years go by, you can display these collages in a hall or move them to an album.

2. Do you have a special birthday coming up in your family...someone's 30th or 40th or 75th? If so, look through your stacks of photos for pictures with that person in them. If you can, find 30 or 40 or even 75 pictures of the honoree, depending on the birthday being celebrated. Put those in a collage or album. On the back of each picture, note all the pertinent information you have (date of photograph, people in the photograph, setting). Consider putting some of this information in captions. By the way, if you don't have enough pictures of your own, ask others in the family to contribute.

3. Although surprise parties can be a lot of fun...especially for the hosts and guests...sometimes the honoree likes to look forward to a special birthday celebration. You can still add elements of surprise in the party itself and even give the guests an active role to play. In the invitation, ask guests to write down one little-known fact they know about the honoree. You can even specify topics ("Childhood," "Favorite Subjects," "Something the Honoree Got Away With," "Contests," "Hometown Adventures," "How the Honoree and Spouse Got Together"). At the party, the surprise program is guests presenting their information in a "This Is Your Life" review, which you can tape and later give to the honoree.

4. Looking for a fun party activity that focuses on an adult honoree? Make a crossword puzzle that captures key events, interests/hobbies and people in the honoree's life. Have guests complete the puzzle as part of the entertainment. You don't have to make up the crossword puzzle yourself. Instead, consult Web resources by typing "creating crossword puzzles" into any search engine.

5. For a family member who is entering a new decade, host a "Welcome to the Decade" party. Put the partygoers "in the spirit" by asking them to dress for the decade. For example, if the honoree is turning 60, guests can dress in attire reminiscent of the 1960s.

6. Looking for an almost effortless way to entertain party guests, honor someone special and participate in a history lesson?
Then host a Question/Answer Party. Let the guests ask the honoree questions and record/videotape the responses. This easy, intergenerational activity is a great way for younger family members to learn about their heritage.

Will the Real Mabel Paulus Please Stand Up?

Milestone birthdays present special opportunities, and Jan Roberts decided to take advantage of one when her mother, Mabel Paulus, turned 90. "I wanted to celebrate Mother's life, so I wrote a script and involved all of Mother's descendants in the presentation. The script was modeled on the popular television game show of the 1950s 'To Tell the Truth.'" (For those of you who did not grow up watching this show, it is referenced in the present-day movie "Catch Me If You Can.")

"One facet I knew I had to capture was Mother's pride in her appearance. She has always 'put herself together' each morning—hair, make-up, jewelry, and 'nylons.' I got my son and two of my sons-in-law to dress up as Mother—wig, make-up, jewelry, and accessories. Their wives created 'skirts' to compliment their shiny blouses. What made this spectacular, however, was the size of these 'Mabels'—the shortest one was 6'3". On cue, each one stepped forward and proclaimed: 'My name is Mabel Paulus.' The host of the game show, another son-in-law, asked each of the contestants questions, and their responses told the story of Mother's life."

Jan continues, "Mother absolutely loved it; we all had fun. The great grandchildren were fascinated and thoroughly entertained."

What are some of your favorite television shows that feature contestants? How can you adapt that format for your family entertainment and stories? Who are your family's "American Idols," and what "Fear Factors" have family members overcome?

The Numbers Game

Looking for an easy way to unify a collection of photos, wishes or memories? If so, play "The Numbers Game." Take the number of the birthday you are celebrating and let it drive the number of items in your gift. For example, let's say you want to honor someone special on that person's 30th birthday. Here's how you can play "The Numbers Game."

- Send a mailing to 30 people. Include a self-addressed, stamped post card. Ask everyone to write a message or a memory of the honoree on the card. As the post cards come back to you, put them in an album. You can present this collection on the honoree's 30th birthday.
- Collect 30 photographs of the honoree. Make a collage or put them in an album. Enhance the photographs with written memories they spark.
- Collect 30 wishes for the honoree. Present them at the party.
- If you are the custodian of your children's essays and artwork saved over the years, collect 30 of these for a 30th birthday album that's a *Family Original.*™
- List 30 attributes of this loved one and then put them in alphabetical order. Create an album with one page per attribute. Tell a story or feature a photograph capturing each attribute.

My Life Story Weekend

"For my birthday I have a special request," Miriam Reeder told her adult children. "I want a weekend for my family to gather and talk." She got all that and much, much more. So did the rest of her family.

They selected an inn that offered them a private meeting room—a neutral setting where no one was responsible for hosting the others. "After everyone arrived on Friday night, we had dinner and then established the rules. They were simple… no taping and no interruptions so the person talking would not be intimidated and could talk as long as they wanted. Only when they were finished could people ask questions.

"We drew for order and began the next morning. It was absolutely amazing. Nobody wanted to stop. The storytelling went until 3 o'clock in the morning. Never before had we listened to each other the way that we did that weekend. I wish we'd done this years ago."

You may have family members who would find this idea appealing but have simply never thought of it. Why don't you suggest it?

BIRTHDAYS

Bench Marks

"For my father-in-law's 80th birthday, I wanted him to know how special he is to his entire family," says Louise Slater. "I also wanted to link our memories with something everyone associates with him. Then it hit me: his tool kit was his 'signature item.' I decided to ask everyone to bring a memory linked to tools…like 'the day you hit the nail on the head' or 'something you hammered home.' At the party, guests read their memories and then put them in a specially decorated album. The 'icing on the cake' was the birthday cake itself. I had it made from a photograph of Papa in his workshop." (You can do the same thing with a favorite photograph. Consult your telephone directory for bakeries that will make a "photograph cake" for your party.)

The book of memories has continued to be a source of joy and gratitude for the family. "What surprised me," Louise said, "is the way everybody got into this and revealed not only their own side of Papa but also their unique way of communicating their relationship with him. This gift is something we gave Papa, and it is also something we gave each other and ourselves."

Who in your family has a major birthday on the horizon? What is that person's "signature item"? How can you link that item and memories of the person you are honoring?

What I Really, Really Like About the Birthday Person

Diane Pryor has a wonderful way to celebrate family birthdays. First the honoree gets to select the menu regardless of the combination. During the meal, everyone takes turns telling the honoree something they "really, really like" about him or her. No one is ever too young or too old for this kind of affirmation.

Imagine the *Family Original™* you could preserve for each person: the menu, the table, the guests, and all the personal affirmations. Recording such memories is not only fun for the person you are honoring but also inspires and instructs future generations.

Use Your Birthday as an Opportunity

Want to make your own extraordinary wish come true? Use your birthday to make it happen. Georgia West wanted to go on a trip to celebrate her 70th birthday. As a contemporary grandmother, she used the Internet to research and plan it. "I saw this milestone in my life as an opportunity for an extraordinary family vacation. I got on the Internet and planned an 11-day excursion. My four children, their spouses and my seven grandchildren (ages 3–13 at the time) signed on. I kept a journal, and each family member made a photo album with their memories. Everybody enjoyed it so much my husband and I are planning another family trip to celebrate our 50th wedding anniversary."

Think about turning your next birthday into an opportunity for getting special people together.

As a new millennium approaches,
For Bob and Caroline age encroaches
Because they're marking a special birthday
(Their 50 years upon-the-earth day!)

So it seems to fit their style
To have a party in the wild
With elephants, zebras, lions, giraffes,
Hors d'oeuvres and spirits, lots of laughs,
For turning 50, how to do it?
For Bob and Caroline, let's just zoo it!

Please, **no presents** and no pranks,
But come on out to Riverbanks.
And pay attention to one feature:
Do come dressed as your favorite creature.
Or if that idea you are loathing,
Then come dressed in safari clothing.

So mark this date for which you're beckoned:
It's January 22nd.
The Reptile Complex is the place
For "party animals" in this case.
From 7:30 to 10:30, and don't forget it,
But call us if you must regret it.

Lucie Eggleston 254-0999
Bill Crosswell 782-5528

© 1993 THE PAPER COMPANY XLSOC70-299

Try This...

What are your five most memorable birthdays? Jot a quick list. Then note why those birthdays stand out. You have just started chronicling some of your life stories.

_____
_____
_____
_____
_____
_____
_____
_____
_____
_____
_____
_____
_____
_____
_____
_____
_____
_____
_____
_____
_____
_____
_____
_____
_____
_____
_____

You don't have to be a child to be honored with a birthday party. In fact, adults will get into the spirit of a costume party if the costume is something they already have in their closets. This "Turning 50—Safari, So-goody" theme party was even held at the zoo. The crowd turned into "party animals," and the pictures prove it.

Anniversaries & Weddings

Anniversaries and weddings are chapters in the bigger story and stories in themselves. These milestones spark memories and focus on commitment. That's why they are natural resources for *Family Originals.*™

For a couple, your anniversary is the one day of the year that is uniquely yours. You may mark it by celebrating the same way each year. You may blend tradition and variety. For example, you might go away for your anniversary but change the destination each year. For major anniversaries such as the 25th or the 40th, couples often enlarge the circle, or their children host a gathering. However you mark the date, be sure to mark the memory.

Have Fun with "The Numbers Game" to Celebrate an Anniversary

We are using the number 10 to illustrate, but you can use these ideas for any anniversary.

■ Here are two simple ideas that cost almost nothing and mean absolutely everything.

For your 10th anniversary, make a list of 10 attributes of your spouse, and entitle it: **"Ten Reasons I Love and Respect You."** Your own handwriting makes this gift even more personal. The list can be on a pretty sheet of paper. You'll be surprised how many more attributes you'll think of; you'll also be touched by the response you'll get.

The second idea is to list 10 special moments in your marriage, and describe them in phrases or paragraphs. Forget structure; forget sequence. List these moments in your handwriting as they come to mind and memory. You will find yourself enjoying reliving special times, and realizing how much you and your spouse share.

■ Overwhelmed by photographs from trips that never made it to an album? Don't despair. Instead, use your favorites in an inspired anniversary present. Create an album that is linked to the anniversary number…in this case, 10. Devote a couple of pages each to 10 trips. Entitle the collection **"The First Ten Years: Ten Stops Along the Way."**

Instead of an album, you can make a collage with the same title and focus. Be sure to identify the destination and year for each photograph.

■ Stop for a moment and list the major milestones in your marriage: the day you got promoted; the day you moved into your new house; the day your first child was born. For a meaningful anniversary gift, put together a collage or album around the milestones. You'll be reminded of all you have built together.

Anniversaries & Weddings

Ideas!

1. Have you ever opened a drawer, box or closet to face...once again...those photographs from your engagement and wedding you always meant to put in an album? Don't despair. It's almost better that you've waited until now to do something with them. Take those neglected pictures and put them in an album to give your spouse on your next anniversary. You can entitle it "The Second Time Around," "Take Two," or "Second Look."

2. Is there a family wedding dress "hanging out" in a closet that's not in mint condition? Here's an idea for preserving it and creating an heirloom gift in the process. Consider using pieces of the dress in a coverlet, quilt or pillows. Look in your local telephone directory under "Quilting" to check out available resources in your area for this kind of potential heirloom. Also type in "quilting supplies" in any search engine on the Web. You'll be surprised at the number of options you'll have for creating an extraordinary anniversary or wedding gift for a family member.

3. How many times have you hosted a party for a bride and groom or an anniversary couple without knowing the people on the guest list? Here's a way to connect a crowd as you honor another couple. We call it a "Connect the Dots" party. All you need is a guest list from the honorees, a bulletin board with pre-drawn circles—or "dots"—and an indelible marker. In your invitation, ask guests to bring a picture or memory of the couple being honored.

As people come in, they can put their picture or memory in a "dot." As the party goes on, a spontaneous storyboard is being created for the couple. At some point, ask the couple being honored to "connect the dots" for the whole crowd. In the process, people at the party will, no doubt, discover their own connections. The bulletin board becomes a gift for the honorees.

4. For a silver or golden wedding anniversary (25th or 50th), write to members of the wedding party and ask them to write a letter to the bride and groom highlighting a memory of their wedding. Surprise the honorees by presenting these letters to them as a collection.

5. An inspired groom wrote all the guests before his wedding and asked them to send their advice for a happy marriage. He created an album of this collected wisdom as a gift to his bride. Responses ranged from "Have dual controls on the electric blanket" to "Don't let the sun go down on your anger."

You can adapt this idea by hosting an "advice shower" for a bride and groom. On the invitation, ask guests to bring written advice they can "present" at the shower. You can collect the advice in an album and ask guests to sign their names, and note how long they have been married.

6. Start your favorite bride and groom off with the gift of family history. Distribute fabric squares and markers to friends and family members, asking each person to write a message to the bride and groom. Turn the squares into a quilt to present to the bride and groom. You can find resources for making this kind of memory quilt on the Web by typing in "memory quilts" in any search engine. Also consult your local telephone directory for quilters and quilting supplies.

7. Looking for a simple way to connect generations on their wedding day? Frame a collection of pictures of different generations wearing the same dress, veil or piece of jewelry. You are reflecting continuity in the midst of change.

Another version of this idea is to apply the concept of "Same Picture Over Time." Do you have pictures of different couples cutting the cake, leaving the reception or making toasts? Select one such standard pose and frame all versions of that picture.

Son of a Preacher Man

If you were to make a collection of musical memories, what songs would you include? When Walt and Katy Barron married in 2002, they made a "Wedding CD," a collection of their musical memories to share as a gift for their guests. Their selections reflected their childhood, courtship and wedding.

1. You are the Sunshine of my Life - Stevie Wonder
2. Leader of the Band - Dan Fogelberg
3. Bushel and a Peck - Guys & Dolls
4. Fly me to the Moon - Frank Sinatra
5. Just You and Me - Chicago
6. Nice Work if You Can Get It - Sting
7. Lovely Day - Bill Withers
8. Brandy - Looking Glass
9. Don't You Want Me, Baby? - Human League
10. Jessie's Girl - Rick Springfield
11. Come on, Eileen - Dexy's Midnight Runners
12. Dancing Queen - The Yayhoos
13. Dixieland Delight - Alabama
14. Ain't Nothin' About You - Brooks & Dunn
15. Rocky Top - Phish
16. Believe Me - Elvis Presley
17. Son of a Preacher Man - Dusty Springfield
18. Love Will Keep Us Together - Captain and Tennille
19. You Make Me Feel Like Dancing - Leo Sayer
20. Moments With You - Gran Torino
21. Summertime - The Sundays
22. Did I Shave My Legs for This? - Deana Carter

June 15, 2002

A bride and groom's first dance is always a meaningful song. Walt and Katy chose "You are the Sunshine of My Life." Walt says, "We chose it because we had been dating for five years before we got married, and there is a line in this song that says: 'It feels like this is the beginning, though I've known you a million years.' This line is cheesy but appropriate in describing Katy and me."

As the son of a Presbyterian minister, Walt included "Son of a Preacher Man." He is quick to say, "I have always loved this song not only because of its catchy tune but also because I always thought it was written about me."

Other selections vary from songs that are a tribute to Walt's southern roots to the country favorite of Katy and her friends, "Did I Shave My Legs for This?" The CD also features several traditional wedding songs. "We included 'Fly Me to the Moon' because every wedding CD should have some Sinatra."

An unusual but poignant number is "Bushel and a Peck." Walt adds, "I chose this for my dance with Mom because she used to sing it to me when I was a little boy. At the wedding, the band said this was the first time they'd ever gotten a request for this number."

Just as the songs reflect memories, the cover evokes yesteryear with the childhood pictures of Katy and Walt.

"Wedding CDs are very common now, but we thought we were on the cutting edge way back in 2002." And they were. The CD was a huge hit and ties family and friends to a wonderful couple and their special event. It is, indeed, Walt and Katy's *Family Original.*™

Stops Along the Way

Take a lesson from Eunice and Randy Meyer if you want to get away from the office. This globe-trotting couple has sunned on the beaches of Bali, traveled through the Khyber Pass in Afghanistan and climbed the Great Wall of China. Best of all, they've always taken their camera.

To honor their 35th wedding anniversary, Eunice reflected on all their adventures. Then she selected her favorite pictures from those places for an album. She entitled the album "Stops Along the Way — 1969 to 2004."

Eunice's presentation of this album to Randy was the surprise element at a gathering of close friends on that anniversary.

Although the album was an anniversary gift for Randy, it turned out to be a gift of memories for Eunice as well. If you were to visit the Meyer home today, you would see this album prominently displayed on their den coffee table.

Anniversaries & Weddings

MEXICO WEDDING

Mr. and Mrs. James Edwin Belser
announce the marriage of their daughter
Sarah Mikell
to
Jere Duncan Eggleston
Lieutenant, United States Marine Corps
on Tuesday the fifth of December
nineteen hundred and forty four
Columbia, South Carolina

Circle of Unbroken Memories

At a gathering of senior citizens at a church in Tennessee, everyone was asked to bring one picture from their wedding. That was the only requirement. Some brought formal posed professional pictures; others brought snapshots. Everyone sat at circular tables in groups of six. Their instructions were simple: "Show your picture, pass it around and allow everyone else to make a comment. Start with the person who has the first birthday in the calendar year."

"I couldn't believe it." the minister recalls. "In less than a minute, there was a loud hum of voices in the room. We had allotted 20 minutes for this part of the program. However, it just took off. An hour-and-a-half later, I told everybody I had to leave for a meeting, but they could keep talking. I'm not sure they even noticed when I left. Pictures were still circulating, and there was a lot of laughter…a lot of bonding, too."

Try a similar activity with family and friends. Host a gathering, and ask each person to bring a picture from a wedding, camp or vacation, or any other theme — pets, cars, costumes. Consider recording the stories on audio or videotape.

Do you remember when you, too, thought the bride was a "princess"? This classic picture captures that magical moment for one 5-year-old.

TO: Andrew M.
FROM: Lizzy G.
There are so many reasons I love you!
YOU ARE...

In the 19th century, Elizabeth Barrett Browning wrote her famous love poem, "How do I love thee? Let me count the ways." Fast forward to the 21st century and another Elizabeth, whose love poem to her husband Andy is actually a photo album she gave him on their 7th anniversary. The opening page is shown above. Elizabeth Cloud's "counting the ways" was made by filling album pages with pictures and attributes showing "the many reasons I love you."

Try This...

Here's a quick idea. Go through your pictures in drawers and boxes as well as the bookshelves and tables of your home. Select any five of you and your spouse. As you pick up each one, jot down your first thoughts. This gives you a head start on your next anniversary gift.

_____

_____

_____

_____

_____

_____

_____

_____

_____

_____

_____

_____

_____

_____

_____

_____

_____

_____

_____

_____

_____

Graduations

Graduations are poignant milestones, an ending and a beginning, not only for the graduate but also for the entire family.

Ten Gallon Hats, Cell Phones and the Domino Effect

When Travis Meyer graduated from Stanford University, he wanted his parents to be able to see him and photograph him in the sea of black mortarboards.

"My friends and I decided we would find a way to distinguish ourselves in the crowd. Those of us from Texas brought along our 'cowboy hats.' We also thought it would be fun to cut out white dots and attach them to our robes so that we looked like a set of dominoes. The final guarantee for having  our families find us in the stadium was to use our cell phones to let our folks know the yard line and side of the field where we were standing."

From the picture it is obvious that Travis' parents were able not only to see him but to photograph him for wonderful graduation memories.

Here's a historical postscript. Along with Travis' mother and father, former President Bill Clinton and Senator Hilary Rodham Clinton were proud parents attending this graduation.

Graduations

Ideas!

1. Looking for a place to store assorted items? Even better, looking for a personal gift for your graduate? Then gather personal items belonging to the graduate—jewelry, badges, foreign coins, possibly a needlepointed purse or pin cushion, maybe a prized knife—and arrange them in a shadow box. To complete this personal gift, include your memories of those items and their connection to your graduate.

2. Do you have assorted photographs of the graduate at various stages in life? If so, put them in an album, and note the memories you associate with the photographs. Put a photograph of your graduate—in cap and gown—on the cover. You can organize other pictures around any of the following themes.

- Favorite moments
- Friends
- Family
- Activities
- Hobbies
- Sports
- Faith
- Achievements and Awards

Enhance the album by getting others to contribute their photographs and memories. If you have school papers or artwork you have saved, think about including selections.

3. Who are the important people in your graduate's life? Make an audio or videotape for the graduate with those friends and family members. You may want to include teachers and advisors. Ask them to recall stories about the graduate that stand out in their memory.

4. Written words can outlive us and preserve our thoughts and feelings. Here's a simple, powerful idea for young parents. Write a letter to your children when they enter the first grade. Let them know your joys, hopes and dreams as parents. Give that letter to them the day they graduate from high school.

Of course, you can write another letter on their graduation day. Think about approaching this message from your perspective of "looking back, looking forward."

Boxes from Home

Sometimes the best gifts are ones we don't even realize we're giving. Without knowing it, Missie McCarty gave a weekly graduation gift to her son Scott. When he entered West Point, the Parents' Club encouraged parents to mail their sons an occasional package. Missie took the message to heart. In fact, she didn't miss a single week. "Sometimes I sent newspaper articles. Sometimes I sent mail. Some packages contained cookies or Band-Aids® for his blistered feet. On Graduation Day I was amazed when more than 25 cadets looked me up to tell me how much they had enjoyed those weekly packages." Apparently, every time a box with her exquisite handwriting arrived, Scott's friends had paid attention. Each box triggered memories of home.

Missie followed the same weekly ritual when her daughter Molly went to UVA. "Molly's packages might include an Ann Landers column, a copy of *Glamour*, hand cream, a sweater, or maybe even homemade cookies."

The impact carried beyond graduation. At the wedding of one of Molly's college friends, the bride told Missie, "I was so touched and excited when the wedding gift arrived. It was my turn to receive a box with your beautiful handwriting. I started thinking of college days when Molly would open her weekly box from home, and all of us in the sorority would take a peek. We almost felt like we'd gotten a package, too."

Wrapped in Memories

Meredith Lind Turner loves wrapping up in her memories of college. University students are famous for collecting t-shirts which commemorate a sorority/fraternity party, a special college event or a fund-raising activity. For a graduation gift, Meredith's mother Patricia Lind asked Meredith to select several of her favorite t-shirts from her four years at the University of Texas. Her mother then called the quilting guild in her hometown and found someone to transfer the decorative logos from Meredith's t-shirts into a patchwork of memories for her.

You can check your laundry for t-shirts that advertise pieces of your graduate's life: organizations, events, causes, activities, vacation stops, slogans. You can turn these into a quilt. Consult your local telephone directory under "Quilting" or type "t-shirt quilts" in any search engine on the Web to check out resources that will make the quilt with the t-shirts you send.

Try This...

Think of the most memorable graduation you've attended. It can be your own, of course. Jot down the first five thoughts that come to mind. Now think of someone special who is graduating. Write that person a note and reference some of your own memories. You will be amazed at how much that kind of personal message means.

_____

_____

_____

_____

_____

_____

_____

_____

_____

_____

_____

_____

_____

_____

_____

_____

_____

_____

_____

REUNIONS

Reunions are a popular way to celebrate the gift of connection and memory, be it high school or college, clubs, camp, or family. If your family doesn't have a reunion on the horizon, think about introducing the idea. Then gauge the response. For all you know, everyone is just waiting for somebody else to mention the possibility. Significant birthdays, anniversaries and holidays can prompt a gathering of the entire clan.

Planning a reunion can be a rich journey in itself, and it's never been easier. Book stores are full of helpful resources. The computer has lifted the burden of maintaining mailing lists, and e-mail offers instant access to information sharing. The key is having a "contact person" in each branch who is responsible for communication with a designated group.

To find worlds of information about planning family reunions, just type "planning family reunions" into any search engine on the Web; click "search" and get ready for a flood of resources.

Eric LeRoach signs in — Sam Davis looks on. Bill's grandson looks on. Gay Davis shakes hands with Ed Alt.

Lewis Ladies — Robin & Dodge Dog Catherine & Susan

Eric worked for months to plan the Camp Davis Reunion at the Foxworth Ranch in Newcastle, Texas (near Graham, Tx.)

Jackie Davis mans the Sign-in table. Betsy & John Bolton

Where did these folks come from, and why are they here?

We are drawn to remember and record places that tell our stories. Often the people who frequent the same place become a kind of "family." Such a place is Camp Davis in the hills of northern New Mexico.

"I can't remember a time Camp Davis wasn't in my life and in my blood," says one camper. "In the late 1940s my father began a summer tradition of transporting our family across west Texas and New Mexico along with our laundry and supplies for a month. In the early days, a dirt road separated Camp Davis from civilization, and what awaited us was a wilderness experience long before wilderness trips were marketed."

Those who love Camp Davis keep returning and introducing it to their children and grandchildren.

That deep connection and loyalty were apparent at the first-ever Camp Davis Reunion held 60 years after the camp's founding. It was a time for sharing stories and memories. Former campers brought their scrapbooks, their tales and their pictures.

One camper from the '50s brought her husband who had climbed mountains all over the world but had never been to Camp Davis. This mountaineer, author and world traveler was struck by the spirit of the crowd: "I am amazed that so many people have come so far to remember a little camp in a remote place and time. This must be some special camp."

What's the "some special place" in your life that's inseparable from who you are...your own "Camp Davis"? Tell its story.

As a rite of passage, campers write their names on the walls each year. The legacy lives on as Caroline Beutel "signs in."

A gathering of immediate family becomes a reunion when family members from near and far share holidays and vacations. Grandparents, aunts and uncles get to enjoy the little people in the family. Likewise, the next generation makes connections they will carry into adulthood.

Nothing dates you like a picture. Just look at these ladies enjoying a college reunion in the late '70s and notice hemlines, shoes and hairstyles. More important, they are living the 3Rs of reunions: reconnecting, reminiscing and refueling…seizing the opportunity to look back while moving forward.

When grandparents Jackie and Sam Davis planned their vacation, it turned into a family reunion. They had a family t-shirt made for all members to wear, and the required group picture spontaneously became a "Kodak® moment". They were so pleased they featured the photograph on their annual holiday card.

A Grandmother's Legacy

All of us want our lives to have purpose, and Leonora Montgomery is a living example of what "purpose" can look like. This mother of four and grandmother of 12 says, "My self-assigned task in life is to see that my grandchildren know each other and love each other. That's not easy since they live in different places. So as a new millennium approached, while everyone else focused on computers and Y2K, I decided I'd seize this moment in history to get all 12 of my grandchildren—ages 4 to 24—together."

That's exactly what she did in June 2000.

"The weekend itself was incredible, but so was the year of planning that led up to it. All of the grandchildren got in the act in one way or another through phone conversations, e-mails and even meetings in various cities where different ones lived. It was *well-organized.*"

One highlight was the grandchildren's response to the obituary Leonora read of her great grandfather. "They sat rapt as I read of his walking from Ohio to Indiana. All of his earthly belongings were on his back. After much hard work, he finally earned enough money to purchase a horse. That very first day his new purchase was struck and killed by lightning. He lost his entire wealth. Through many hardships he continued to persevere and build a new life. Later he became a land-owner and a member of the state legislature. I chose to read all that to show my grandchildren how they are descended from very strong stock…that spirit is in their blood."

The extraordinary weekend together culminated in a Sunday service on the dock. This grandmother and her 12 grandchildren sat outside in their sweaters in the cool Maine morning and talked about their spiritual growth over the last few years. They closed by singing songs together.

Reflecting on the experience, Leonora says,"I had four reasons for doing this:

1. to get all the grandchildren together *alone with me*;
2. to talk with my grandchildren and *see the future through their young eyes*;
3. to tell them about their family and *their connection* to their past;
4. to inspire them to embrace their family's values and their heritage in the future.

"The weekend was all that and more. Now as I look at the pictures, I treasure not only the memories, but also the hope they give me for the future."

Here are some easy ways to preserve family stories during a family reunion.

1. Seize the opportunity for identifying orphan memorabilia. Before going, gather your photographs of unknown subjects. During the reunion, make all orphan photographs available so people can contribute information they may have about the photos.

2. Attack those boxes from the attic, and look for letters, essays or speeches that impress you. Reproduce your favorites at a copy store to share. There may be time at the reunion to discuss lessons these documents still teach. Remember that handwriting is part of your personal history and adds authenticity. Scanners and copy machines make it easy to duplicate handwritten treasures.

3. Why don't you tape your own "Prime Time Live" at your family reunion? Before the reunion, consider how you want to use videotaping to record priceless family stories. There may be people in every generation you want to interview on tape. Is there a family member who will volunteer to coordinate the taping of highlights? If not, would you consider hiring that expertise?

4. Musical relatives can take center stage in an original "musical review" of family history. Take familiar tunes and add lyrics that tell your story. You can involve family storytellers, poets and musicians in this activity. Be sure to videotape the production.

5. Here's an easy idea for a family album. Ask one family member to coordinate the creation of this automatic memento. This volunteer provides a scrapbook for each family unit with pre-made pages. Sample titles include "Grandpa," "First Cousins," "Aunts and Uncles," "Parents." At some point in the reunion, each unit takes a picture for each page, and people jot down comments and impressions about the specific relatives. The final page is designated for the group picture.

6. Don't wait for a formal invitation to a family reunion. Plan your own traveling version. Make a list of people to visit, and then mark locations on a map to plan your trip. Take along your camera, your journal and your tape recorder (audio, video, or both). Preserve the experience in an album, as part of a collage or on a tape.

7. Who in your family is Web savvy? Ask that person to extend the spirit of the Family Reunion by starting a family Web page. Go to any search engine and type in "creating Web pages." Information abounds.

Notice that the golden retriever in the foreground did not want to miss out on the picture or the fun of playing with the children on the front row.

The Gathering of the Clan

If you want to perfect the art of a well-honed family reunion, take lessons from the Colby Family. In 2003, the Colby Clan gathered in East Orange, Vermont, for its 50th annual reunion. Here's the announcement from the family newsletter:

Join us in a very rural environment which our Forefathers developed in the 1800s and cherished so much. Relax in the former one-room schoolhouse, visit the village cemetery, or walk about and take photographs. Enjoy lunch as prepared by local residents, attend the annual Business Meeting, and then learn about the rural lifestyle of yesteryear. That is, prior to farm tractors, TV, urban development and the Internet...

The newsletter is a wonderful resource, inspiration and education in itself. Family members contribute $5.00 a year to maintain and expand the communication and to receive invitations to the reunions. The newsletter also provides a forum for sharing information and soliciting family members' input in the research process. Furthermore, older family members, some in nursing homes, are able to keep up with their family connections across the country.

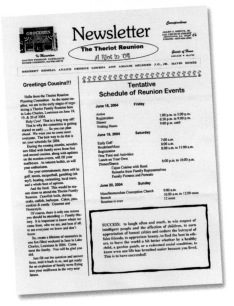

"When the first newsletter arrived, I was very excited to learn that we were having our first family reunion," says Christie Woodfin. "That first newsletter also promised monthly editions during the year before the actual reunion date. What happened was that cousins began connecting long before the reunion. You see, the first newsletter instructed a person from each family unit to write an article about their clan. When family members started submitting stories about what they were doing and where they were living, other family members started contacting them to talk about common interests such as mutual friends, colleges that cousins attended, and similar occupations of aunts and uncles. The stories in the newsletters, therefore, not only brought back wonderful memories and inspired lots of family reflection but they also encouraged connection and reconnection among relatives even before the reunion."

Family Gratitude

"We always close our Family Reunion with a worship service," says Trish McGehee Sargent. "We end by having each person complete this sentence: 'I am thankful for this about my family...'" At future reunions, Trish can tape this part of the service and distribute copies to family members.

Consider including a worship service as part of your next family reunion.

Try This...

List five groups who have played an important role in your life...such as childhood friends, neighbors, band members, sorority sisters, fraternity brothers, scout troops, campers. Opposite each one, write the names of people who were in that group. Put a check mark by those you can get in touch with. Then contact those people to discuss the possibility of getting together. Even if you can't put a date on the calendar, you'll be amazed at the memories you trigger.

_____

_____

_____

_____

_____

_____

_____

_____

_____

_____

_____

_____

_____

_____

_____

_____

_____

_____

_____

Mother's Day and Father's Day

Some people consider Mother's Day and Father's Day commercial promotions. We prefer to think of them as special times to honor mothers and fathers. Besides, if you create a *Family Original,*™ you are focusing on meaning, not materialism.

The Significant Women in My Life

This picture tells a powerful story about the beginning of a new generation. Born prematurely, Louise Slater was given only a 50/50 chance of survival. The spirited baby opted for life. Pictured here at her miraculous homecoming are her mother and both grandmothers.

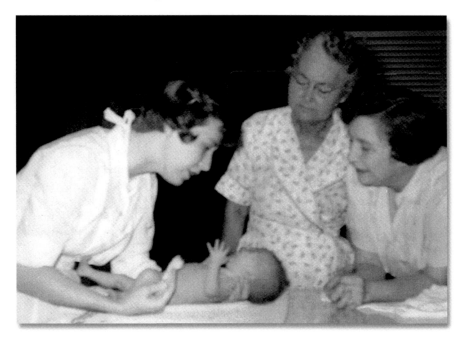

"I look at this picture every morning and think of the three most significant women in my life," says Louise, now 50. "I also think about my friend Sally Boone, who gave me this picture the first Mother's Day after my mother died." Sally's thoughtful sensitivity adds another dimension to this picture of three generations celebrating the gift of life.

What pictures do you have that you can share with mothers and friends on Mother's Day?

Mother's Day and Father's Day

1. Here's a delightful way to thank your mother for her wisdom. Make a list of lessons she taught you. Then put those memories in a collection. You can buy an album and add the stories, or you can put your stories in a journal whose cover and design express the mood and tone of your stories. Tell the stories in your own handwriting.

Set your mind free to roam from philosophical lessons (getting a disappointing grade) to practical ones (getting grease out of your t-shirts). Give it a title page like "Wisdom I Learned from My Mother."

Adapt this idea for others close to you: your father, grandparents, aunts and uncles, and friends.

Here's a real twist on the idea: Mothers...Fathers, jot down a list of lessons you have learned from your children. Start now and write the lessons down as they occur, dating your entries.

2. Want to turn orphaned pictures into a great gift? Isolate all the photos you have of your mother. Put them in an album with your associated memories. If possible, add captions specifying names, date, and location. You might organize the pictures around "The Many Faces of Mama"—comforter, entertainer, hostess, artist, cook, musician, storyteller, disciplinarian. You can create this same gift with pictures of your father—handyman, gardener, fisherman, hunter, golfer, storyteller, musician, cook, advisor, teacher. If you don't have many pictures of your parents, make a list of each parent's "many faces" and illustrate the faces with stories.

3. Here's the perfect gift for the brand-new mother. Frame the baby's birth announcement and accompanying picture. This is also a great Mother's Day gift for the baby's grandmothers.

4. Create a collage of pictures with you and your mother or father. If possible, date them. Add favorite quotes as your captions. The quotes don't have to be from your parents, either.

"Giving birth is little more than a set of muscular contractions granting passage of a child. Then a mother is born."
— Erma Bombeck

Eight is Enough

Question: What do you give your 75-year-old father for Father's Day?
Answer: A *Family Original*™ **collection of memories.**

One of eight siblings sent a stack of eight note cards and the following instructions to her brothers and sisters:

Something fun that's not too hard:
Put a memory on each card.
This is just the thing for Dad.
For Father's Day, and he'll be glad.

The instructions further explained that all eight siblings should mail their memory cards directly to their dad. On Father's Day, he received a flip-able photo album to showcase his children's memories.

One card read: "I remember the Borden's® Ice Cream store near your office where you stopped for popsicles on your way home. When all the children heard you whistling up the walkway, we knew you were bringing popsicles from the ice cream store. To this day, the sound of whistling evokes a happy memory of growing up."

The gift was a hit. "As the cards arrived, I had the best time reading the memories from each of my children," proclaimed the proud father. "I have this thoughtful collection prominently displayed and flip through it all the time. At my age, it's okay to brag on my children and take the time to reflect on my life."

"I'm part of a group that goes away each year for a few days of wonderful conversation and relaxation, and one year I decided to do something special for these five friends," explains Eleanor Barron. "Conscious of the fact that I was the only one whose mother was no longer living, I wrote to the mother of each friend and asked her to write a letter to her daughter about how much she meant to her. I explained that the letter would likely be shared with the five other friends during our time together.

"All five mothers eagerly complied with my request, and I arrived at our retreat with five handwritten letters tied in satin ribbon. I was thrilled to be giving my friends a treasure which they had no idea of receiving, and the experience was even more precious than I had imagined. Within a year, one of the mothers died and a second was soon unable to communicate. Not only does each of my friends have her letter to cherish, we as a group have the memory of this shared experience."

Mother's Day and Father's Day

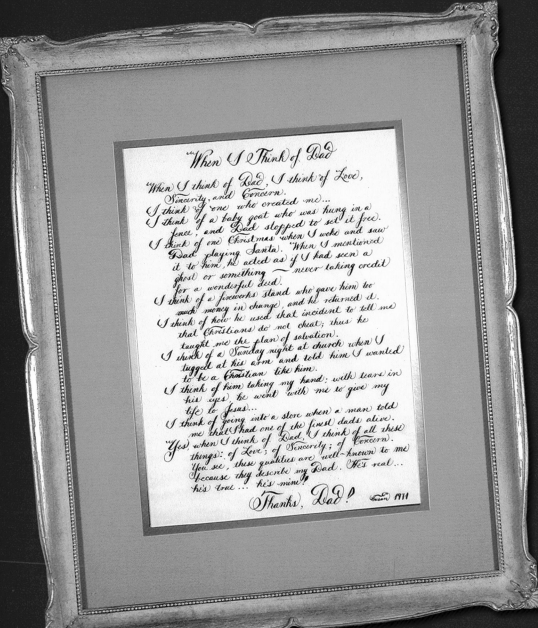

When I Think of Dad

When I think of Dad, I think of Love,
Sincerity, and Concern.
I think of one who created me...
I think of a baby goat who was hung in a
fence, and Dad stopped to set it free.
I think of one Christmas when I woke and saw
Dad playing Santa. When I mentioned
it to him, he acted as if I had seen a
ghost or something — never taking credit
for a wonderful deed.
I think of a fireworks stand who gave him too
much money in change, and he returned it.
I think of how he used that incident to tell me
that Christians do not cheat; thus he
taught me the plan of salvation.
I think of a Sunday night at church when I
tugged at his arm and told him I wanted
to be a Christian like him.
I think of him taking my hand; with tears in
his eyes he went with me to give my
life to Jesus...
I think of going into a store when a man told
me that I had one of the finest dads alive.
Yes, when I think of Dad, I think of all these
things: of Love; of Sincerity; of Concern.
You see, these qualities are well-known to me
because they describe my Dad. He's real...
he's true... he's mine!
Thanks, Dad!
Susan 1971

Dear Dad

People often let you know when it's okay to go public with their letters. Susan Murphey certainly did. Her freshman year in college, she wrote her father a letter recalling special times they had shared, business dealings that reflected his integrity and lessons he had taught by example. Later, as a gift to her father, Susan had a cousin print the letter in calligraphy. Then she framed it. When her father died, Susan moved this tribute of a life well-lived from his wall to hers. His influence lives on.

So does Susan's. Without realizing it, Susan inspired her daughter Morgan when she went off to school. Morgan wrote her own father a similar letter of tribute and gratitude.

Letters are lasting gifts. As this story illustrates, these tangible expressions of love and connection can also link several generations.

Why don't you write a letter to your own parents this Mother's Day and Father's Day?

A Mother's Graduation

Usually a graduate's parents pop with pride during Commencement. In this case, though, the children are applauding their graduating Mama. With incredible support from her husband and children, Laurie Carter Tharpe fulfilled her lifelong dream of becoming a doctor. At age 39, Laurie started medical school, and the weekend she graduated, so did her son Carter...from high school, that is. She is no longer the only Dr. Tharpe in the family, either. Two of her children have gone on to become doctors themselves.

If you are looking for a way to honor your parents on Mother's Day or Father's Day, think of ways they have inspired you to fulfill your dreams. As a gift, write them a letter of thanks. If you have a picture such as this one to trigger the memory, consider framing it along with your tribute.

Fathers and Feathers

"On Father's Day I often reminisce about my days as an Indian Princess," says "Little Feather." By design, the YMCA Indian Princess program creates opportunities for fathers and daughters to spend time together at monthly meetings, overnight camp-outs and special events such as Derby Day.

"I still have my Indian Princess headband, my Indian Princess necklace, my winning Derby Day car, many wonderful pictures, and priceless memories of our times together," she continues. "For my next Father's Day card, I have decided to write a poem about all our adventures in Indian territory."

Try This...

Divide a sheet of paper in half. Label one side "Mother" and the other, "Father." Then under each heading, list people—other than family members—who know that parent well. This is the first step in a wonderful gift for each parent. Plan to contact each person on the list to record their stories about your parents. The gift itself can be a collection of memories from significant people in your parents' lives.

_____
_____
_____
_____
_____
_____
_____
_____
_____
_____
_____
_____
_____
_____
_____
_____
_____
_____
_____

Houses

If houses could talk, they would tell great stories. The farm houses, ranch houses, vacation houses, tree houses, dog houses, doll houses, and play houses of our lives are a rich source of family history. Forget addresses such as 1600 Pennsylvania Avenue or #10 Downing Street, and revisit the addresses of your life, this time from the point-of-view of the stories those places house.

Blue Willow Collected on Blue Willow

"I started collecting Blue Willow china the year Jess and I married," says Betty Tutor, "because our first house was on a street named Blue Willow. We've been married 30 years, and this collection has been with us the whole time. I keep adding pieces to the display that links the chapters of our lives."

Houses

365 Upper Mountain Ave, Upper Montclair, NJ

1st house in Columbia lived here when Bob was born

A simple way to arrange pictures—either in a scrapbook or in a collage—is to put a picture of your house at the top of the page. Other pictures on this page or in the collage can then reflect life lived at this address.

Another idea for a page or a collage is to group pictures of various houses in a family's life.

Building or Remodeling?

Chronicle the process. By all means, take "before and after" shots—of the house *and* of the people who are living through the process. Record your thoughts and feelings on videotape or in an album with your photographs.

Start Work on New Herrick Home

which requires only a touch of the finger instead of pressing or flicking a switch.

Guild Electric has contract for the wiring and McGregor's for the plumbing.

Construction on the new home of Mr. and Mrs. Harold W. Herrick, at the northeast corner of Cherry, was started th R. J. Smith, general co Of native stone w block partitions, the h "L" shaped with the Tenth and the wing along the Cherry stre will form two sides of flower garden on the the lot which is 150 Included in the ho large living room, din glass walls opening library, two bedroo room, sewing room, ity and bath rooms. tached. Heating will be in the floor, with t and hot water hea Floors will be of For the first tim is believed, two being used: Mode touch light switc fold back into the opening out or sliding into walls. Electric lights will be turned on and off through the "touch plate"

History in the Making

"It was such an amazing Christmas gift." says Bertie Bond. "Kate and I still can't get over it. When we opened that box to find the counted cross-stitched picture of our home, we were stunned. Apparently, Julia Gary and Mollie Merrick had been planning this gift for two years."

Julia is quoted as saying, "I couldn't do the needlework, but I could provide the financing. Mollie does exquisite needlework, so we teamed up to give this special Christmas present. First we took a picture of the house. Then Mollie took the picture to the local needlepoint shop. The shop sent the picture off to England and had the pattern drawn with appropriate colors. It took Mollie two years to stitch it because it has over 25,000 stitches. The secrecy surrounding the gift played a great part in the fun and anticipation," says Julia. "When the picture was finished, we could hardly wait to frame and wrap it."

Because this home is located in the Historic District of Decatur, Georgia, this gift of friendship and generosity also tells a great story of historic preservation.

Houses

1. Start with the house you live in, and take people on a home tour...on videotape, that is. Involve the entire family. Go first to the room you enjoy most as a family—most likely the den, kitchen or FROG. "Tell on" the room—what comes to mind about this area? Then record each family member in their special space in the house. This kind of tape not only records family life at this point, but it makes a fun family gift for relatives who live far away.

2. Host a "Friends and Foundation" party during a building project. Invite those closest to you to write a message on the foundation or studs, forever linking home and loved ones. Videotape the ritual, asking guests to read their messages. Take photographs to include in an album that tells the story of your home.

3. Here's a simple idea. Make a list of all the places you have lived. If you have pictures of all of them, create a collage, and note the actual addresses and dates you lived there.

4. Location. Location. Location. Create an album, and call it "Family Address Book."
At the top of each page, put a "house picture." Devote the rest of the space to pictures of people and activities you associate with that location. Be sure to note your memories.

5. Travel back in time. Revisit—literally—the addresses of your life. Videotape each location, and record your memories of that place and time.

6. Preserve your roots—your plant roots, that is—or something else tangible from the places you have lived. Pass these—and their stories—on to other members of your family. Examples other than plants might be tiles, architectural details, light fixtures, and bricks.

7. For those of you who love gardening and the land, frame botanicals from a place your family has lived. This gift will forever connect your loved ones not only with you but also with the earth.

8. Here's a simple idea for a family gathering. It's also entertaining and educational. Plan an evening of storytelling around the theme of houses. List all the significant addresses in your family history. Put each one on a separate piece of paper. Everyone gets to draw one address from the box and tell their memories of that address. Record the stories.

9. Looking for an extraordinary gift idea for people who have lived a number of places? Make an "address quilt". You can showcase the places of a lifetime for a couple celebrating a major anniversary or a family member celebrating a milestone birthday. This is also a great idea for close friends who are moving away. Let significant people contribute meaningful messages and memories on individual fabric squares.

The next question is, "So how do I make one of these?" Office supply and craft stores sell the fabric and pens. Then again, you don't have to make the quilt yourself. If you'd rather have someone make it for you, simply consult any search engine on the Web for "memory quilts." You'll find many resources.

Another option is a photo quilt. Start by isolating your photos of places you've lived. Then choose the ones you want to turn into squares. Again, office supply and craft stores sell the materials you'll need. You can also have the quilt made. Just type "photo quilts" into any search engine to access Web resources.

Make it Personal

Turn original art of your home into notepaper. For the computer savvy, you can scan the artwork yourself and print. Otherwise, work with a local print shop. You can also use the notepaper for invitations, especially when you are entertaining in your home.

Here's a meaningful gift idea. Frame a sketch of a house that tells a story. Another possibility is framing an architect's drawing of your house.

Try This...

Select five of the following, and jot down your first responses. Have fun! Pick five at random, or read through the list and check the five most appealing ones. Your responses will initiate a collection of "house stories." Now start!

• What are the pivotal houses of your childhood, including your own house, your grandparents' homes and the homes of aunts, uncles and friends?

• What household items stand out in your memory—"Harvest Gold" and "Avocado Green" appliances, shag carpets, black-and-white TV sets, or rotary telephones in the hall?

• Did you have your own room growing up or share a room? Either way, what lessons did you learn?

• Did you write messages on the wall or in a closet? Did your kitchen door hold records of the height of children? What stories come to mind as you reflect on those?

• Where did you play after school?

• Did you have a tree house? A play house? A play room? What memories do they evoke?

• Did you ever have to give up your room for a visitor? What are your memories of those visitors and that household arrangement?

• Who came to visit in your home? Relatives? Friends? Exchange students? What do you remember about those visits?

• Did the garage shelter something other than the car? What stories does your garage tell?

• Were there remodeling projects? Did you ever build a house?

• Did you ever live in an apartment? Where was it? Was it furnished or unfurnished? What memories do you have of your neighbors?

• Did your family have a vacation home or cabin? Did you ever rent a place for vacations?

• What are your memories of house parties?

My Home-grown Memories

1. _____
_____

2. _____
_____

3. _____
_____

4. _____
_____

5. _____
_____

Cars

Are We There Yet?

Family cars, mile markers in a family's history, often take on mythical value. From drive-in movie theatres to confidential talks in the driveway, cars have provided generations far more than mobility. Access to wheels brings status, freedom and adventure…and sometimes even magic, like stuffing seven friends in a four-passenger sedan long before the days of seat belts, cruise control, and fuel efficiency. Because cars are family members, they are entertaining and sentimental "vehicles" for conveying the family stories.

Auto-Biographies

"Look at that!" Bill Timmons said to his wife Connie while on vacation in Hawaii. He was looking at the first stretch limousine he had ever seen and immediately became inspired. Bill and Connie had eight children and, while stretch limo meant luxury to some, it said "family car" to Bill.

When the Timmons returned to Greenville, South Carolina, Bill took his idea to the Oldsmobile dealership where it soon became reality. Bill bought an Oldsmobile, had it cut in half, and added two seats in the middle. The result was his own "stretch car."

King-Sized Car For Happy Family And Friends

MYRTLE BEACH—This eight-door sedan owned by Mr. and Mrs William R. Timmons Jr. had vacationers blinking their eyes along the Grand Strand last week. The Timmonses (standing at rear of the right line) and their eight children were joined in Windy Hill Dr. and Mrs. Frank Stelling (right) and their six children and Mr. and Mrs. Dewey Friddle (center) and their three children, All from Greenville.—(Photo by Myrtle Beach Chamber of Commerce).

Oldsmobile Ninety-Eight Adjusted To Carry 25

Timmons Family's Auto Is 'Stretched Out' To Better Accommodate 8 Kids And 2 Adults

This car made the national news when the family went on their vacation to Windy Hill Beach. A reporter from the Associated Press spotted it and snapped a picture. That picture appeared in newspapers throughout the country.

After the children grew up, Bill gave the car to the high school athletic director in Travelers Rest, South Carolina, who used it to take the tennis team to matches.

That "car" still cruises, especially in the hearts of its passengers.

Ideas!

Cars

A natural medium for preserving car stories is audiotape. After all, we listen in the car…to the radio, to CDs, to books on tape, and to each other. Just think of the fun you can have creating a set of audiotapes of your car stories. Besides, it's a hilarious way to entertain the family on a trip.

A way to start is to list all the cars that have been in your family…from the Model T to the SUV. Then get inspired by the ideas, stories and questions that follow.

1. Hurry and get the stories from the generation that can still tell you about the introduction of the automobile into family life. This is an opportunity to record anecdotal evidence of American history.

2. Create an audiotape or CD of the music you loved to hear in the car. You can organize the selections according to decades or chapters of your life. On your CD cover, include the sentiment behind the selections.

A fabulous gift for a close friend is a tape of the music you both enjoyed. You could entitle this CD "Forever Cruisin'."

If you're a grad from Georgia Tech, you'll know a car named "Ramblin' Wreck"

Georgia Tech alumnus John Lumpkin was proud to stand with his family in front of the famous "Ramblin' Wreck from Georgia Tech" for his Christmas card picture over 20 years ago. The 1930 Ford still leads the Georgia Tech football team onto the field every home game—as it has done since September 30, 1961, when the car was unveiled to a crowd at Grant Field. This icon, a proud "rolling tribute" of the Institute, continues to symbolize the students who proudly sing, "I'm a Ramblin' Wreck from Georgia Tech and a helluva' engineer."

Flames Extinguished and Flames Still Burning

Yes, this red hot car has a red hot story!

A proud groom had planned to whisk his bride off on their honeymoon in his brand new 1968 red Porsche. Mere hours before the wedding, however, one of the groomsmen decided he wanted to take the Porsche for a drive. Somehow, he flooded the engine, and the brand new car burst into flames! With amazingly quick reflexes, the groom grabbed a fire extinguisher and put out the flames soon enough to save the car, but not in time for its intended get-away role.

As the bride tells the story, the groom took care of having the car fixed while they were on their honeymoon, and, in record time, the Porsche resumed its role as the couple's sporty new car.

Those flames in the car might have been extinguished, but not the flames of the young couple—and that red sports car is still with them 35 years later.

We love to name our vehicles—cars, boats and even buses. When this group of Clemson students named their bus "Cheap Seats," little did they know it would lead to more than a view of the game. For at least one of them, it led to romance when a young lady approached William Lamb and asked if all the seats had been taken. He grinned and moved over. And that was the start of their romance.

Fall is a time when teenagers decorate each other's cars and show their joie de vivre as well as their school spirit. Just look at Dana Burns's car. "I love the freedom of driving," says Dana. Although she turned 16 in 2004, her words have been uttered as long as teenagers have had access to cars. Pictured here with her friends Cecile Bishop and Mary Katherine Rebentishch, Dana says proudly, "I have had my license for almost 6 months and haven't had a fender bender or gotten a ticket yet."

May her good fortune continue.

Keep on Truckin'

This destination wedding in New Mexico lends itself to fun, surprise and a touch of local color as the bride and groom entertain friends and family with their "pick-up getaway." By the way, the traditional limousine was waiting just around the corner for final "pick up and delivery."

Cars

Gorilla Tactics

Atop a steep hill at an intersection in Atlanta, Georgia, the Gorilla Car Wash still stands. This prime location was ideal for driving in and out for a quick clean-up. That's why Carolyn Avery stopped there one morning on her way to a funeral. Planning to meet her husband Bill later at the service, Carolyn knew she had plenty of time to get the car washed first. It was not to be.

The story is like an old song; you almost have to hear Carolyn recount the details herself to get the full impact. First, picture Carolyn dressed in her Sunday best—hose, heels and all. Now picture her walking out of the car wash as the attendant waves his towel to indicate that the car is clean and ready to drive off. What happened next was nothing short of amazing…but it is the phone call to her husband Bill that is now famous.

As Carloyn walked to her car, the car began to slowly roll down the hill; the attendant had forgotten to put the emergency brake on. Carolyn tried to grab the car, but was pulled to her knees as she watched the car make its way down the steep hill, cross four lanes of traffic, roll into the Burger King parking lot across the street and, thankfully, avoid hitting any cars or people before it crashed into the side of the restaurant.

Rightfully upset about the car, but more shaken by her torn hose, scraped shoes, ripped dress, and bloody knees, Carolyn called her husband Bill and is quoted as tearfully screaming, "Bill, I'm at the Gorilla Car Wash. My dress is ruined; my hose are torn. The car has just rolled down the hill, crossed four lanes of traffic and crashed into the side of the Burger King."

It is said that Bill just couldn't quite grasp the picture that Carolyn was frantically describing, and besides, Bill didn't even know there was such a thing as the "Gorilla Car Wash." He calmly said, "Carolyn, could you possibly tell me again—more slowly—what's happened?"

Well, the calmer Bill was, the more tearful and upset Carolyn became, as she repeatedly screamed into the phone, "Bill, I'm at the Gorilla Car Wash. My dress is ruined, my hose are torn. The car has just rolled down the hill, crossed four lanes of traffic and crashed into the side of the Burger King."

As Carolyn recounts the tale, it took several repetitions before Bill just finally gave up and exclaimed, "Carolyn, give me an address. I'm coming to get you."

And that's exactly what he did. Fortunately, damage was minor in all categories except Carolyn's equilibrium.

What had begun as a spontaneous stop en route to a funeral ended with a story that has acquired a life of its own and, frankly, gets better with every retelling.

Which of your traffic mishaps have led to great stories?

The Galloping Yellow Capri

First covered wagons headed west, then stage coaches, then trains. They were all preliminaries to the Yellow Capri that won the west in 1974. Shortly after school ended in May, three teachers left Atlanta in the rolling sunbeam pictured to the left. Every time they crossed another state line, they hopped out for a photo. From the Grand Canyon to the World's Fair in Spokane, Washington, the Yellow Capri introduced her three passengers to unbelievable scenery, interesting people and country music. Nine thousand miles and five weeks later, these three teachers crossed the Georgia state line with rolls of undeveloped film, countless memories and precious cargo…Coors beer they had purchased in Colorado to give their closest friends. After all, in 1974, Coors was not distributed east of the Mississippi.

Neiman Marcus, Hats, Heels, Gloves, and a 1940s Hot Rod

"It was such a piece of junk with its broken engine and rusted-out body," says Randy Lewis about his first car, a 1939 Ford. "I paid the guy $35.00 for it, but at age 15, I thought that was a deal. The guy had his dogs tied to it in the front yard.

"I enlisted my brother to help me. When we got the body in a somewhat improved-looking state, we tackled the engine. I went to the Friendly Chevy dealership in Dallas and bought Corvette parts—this hot rod was going to be fast! When we got that car running, it was fast—obscenely fast because the engine was so powerful and the body weighed so little. It was such a hot rod! We used an old wash tub as a seat. There was no muffler, so we were not only fast but loud. My father must have gotten nervous about speed and safety because soon he bought me a 1940 Ford which did indeed have real seats and a complete body. I wanted to keep that fast engine I had built, so I put it in the 1940 Ford and had myself another fast, cool car.

"My older sister Susie was impressed with my wheels and borrowed them to take her friend Cherry King to the Zodiac Room at Neiman Marcus. Susie's legs were too short to reach the gas pedal, so my fast engine would send her lurching forward in the car but backward in her seat; then she would pull herself back up to gas the car again and immediately would fly forward in the car but slide backwards in the seat.

"This lurching paid off, however, when they got admiring glances in the Neiman Marcus parking lot as they emerged from my prized hot rod in their pill box hats, high heels and white gloves."

At first glance, these cars may not look extraordinary, but they tell a story of travel and adventure. The car on the left transported a vacationing couple on their first trip through England and Northern Wales. Two years later the rental car on the right took this couple touring in Tuscany. Pictures of your cars can become a fun part of your travel album, and taking those pictures can become a fun ritual of the trip that keeps your story rolling into the future.

Try This...

Cars

Select five of the following, and jot down first responses. Have fun. Exceed the speed limit.
Pick five at random, or read through the list and check the five most appealing ones.

My Auto-biography

1. _____

_____

2. _____

_____

3. _____

_____

4. _____

_____

5. _____

_____

Ladies and gentlemen, start your engines!

- What's the first car you remember?
  - What are the places it took you?
- Who rode in the car with you?
  - What did you name your cars?
- What are your first vacation memories in the car?
  - How did your parents maintain peace on car trips?
- How many imaginary lines did you draw in the back seat?
  - Who was first to ask, "Are we there yet?"
- What games did you play in the car?
  - What songs did you sing?
- When did you get your first station wagon, van, truck, SUV?
  - What rules did you break in the car?

Why not "park" your favorite car photos in an album or collage? The advantage of an album is you can add your memories. The advantage of a collage is you can hang it in a prominent place for all to see.

- Did you ever go to a drive-in movie?
  - Did you ever "borrow" the car without permission?
- Do you remember your first air-conditioned car?
  - Did your car pull a boat or a trailer?
- Did you have a luggage rack?
  - Where did you park your car—street, driveway, garage?
- When did you become a multi-vehicle family?
  - Did you ever "ride around" and look at the Christmas lights?

- Is there a story about the "getaway car" from a family wedding?
  - Who taught you to drive?
- What do you remember about learning to drive?
  - Think about the day you got your driver's license.
- When and why did you get your first ticket?
  - What lessons did cars teach you about money?
- When did you first get your own car?
  - When did you have your first flat tire?
- Have you ever run out of gas?
  - What are your classic memories of getting lost, asking—or not asking—for directions, taking the wrong turn?

- What memories do you have of car seats—leather, upholstery, bucket, fold-down, back seats, baby seats?
  - Did you have to earn car money, including gas money?
- What do you remember about teaching your children to drive?
  - What are your car "appliances"—cell phones, radar detectors, GPS systems, DVD players?
    - What movies and DVDs are favorites with travelers?
      - What are your favorite books on tape?

  - Attention young parents: How have travel arrangements and entertainment in the car changed since your own childhood? What experiences have remained unchanged?

Pets

Pets narrate powerful stories and become permanent residents in our homes, history and hearts. Pets also teach us truths about responsibility, birth and death, loyalty, companionship, and trust. Consider letting your pet tell your story.

The Happy Life

"Happy was the best gift I ever gave my husband," says Lucie Eggleston of this beloved yellow Lab. "I presented this puppy to him on his 40th birthday, and my birthday present to him the year she died was an album I put together about her extraordinary life. To create the album, I went through envelopes of pictures and pulled every one with Happy in it. In the process of putting the book together, I worked through my grief. I believe the album helped him work through his, too. Happy will live forever in our hearts, and this book will always have a special place in our home."

Pets

Ideas!

1. Go through those envelopes of pictures and separate all those that include pets. Then make an individual stack for each pet. From there, let those pets start talking on album pages or in a collage. Remember there are Web resources you can use for creating your *Family Original.*™ Go to any search engine and type "personal photo albums" or "personal photo collages."

2. Choose 12 favorite pet pictures that correspond with the months and seasons. Take them to a copy store and have a calendar made.

3. Sometimes animals can reach us in places that people can't. Think about your relationship with your pets and take time to record those feelings. You can put them in a booklet or record them on audiotape. To get you started, here are some topics:

- "What I Learned From My Pet"
- "If People Were More Like Their Pets "
- "How Pets Offer Companionship"
- "The Bunny I Won at the Easter Egg Hunt"
- "Cat Lover for Life"
- "My Critter Collection"

4. If you are part of the generation that watched "Lassie," "Old Yeller," or "Bird Man of Alcatraz," you know animals have always made great movie stars. Look at commercials today on television to see how advertisers use animals to evoke emotions that sell products. If you have a pet, then you have a star. Become your own producer and director by having your pet star in your own video.

5. Turn your premiere of this original production into a night of family entertainment. Just add pizza, and you have "dinner and a movie."

6. What are your favorite childhood books and stories about animals? Create a family reading list, and encourage intergenerational conversations. Books on this list make great birthday and Christmas gifts for children. Include an inscription about why you love this book.

You can't choose your relatives, but you can choose your pet. Record this "moment of choice."

For better, for worse—for your Lab, for my Lab

NOEL

My First Pet

I got him as a Christmas present from the Haltiwangers. He was a wonderful first pet. He was and albino, and he had many problems. We think he was both blind and deaf, but I think it made him that much sweeter. He was born on December 20th and lived for about a yeah and a half. While I was at camp one year he got really sick. When I returned I saw him one last time at my grandmothers house, and then he died that night. He is buried on the lakeside of her house in Forest Acres.

Sometimes a school assignment can become a treasured *Family Original*™. What essays do you have about beloved pets and the lessons they teach us?

107.

Pets

WAGS and SPUNKY

by
Opal Curry McKinney

Pet Talk

It's never too late to pursue an interest. Just ask Martye Armstrong about her grandmother, Opal Curry McKinney, who was born in 1887. After one daughter married and the other went to college, Opal took a creative writing course. She then started writing a series of letters from her dog to her daughter's dog. At age 95, Opal published the letters using the names of the dogs in the title: *Wags and Spunky*. Martye says of this *Family Original:* "I love to read the history of my mother and grandmother through the voices of the animals they loved. I also love my grandmother's spirit and lifelong joy of learning. She inspires me still."

October 14

Dear Little Spunky,

Welcome to our family! You are in our family now you know, since you live with Martha and Joe. Your mistress, Martha, lived here with us until she married Joe a few weeks ago. He calls her Snooze because she likes to sleep so well. You'll enjoy being their little puppy. They are grand people and lots of fun.

Martha wrote her mother, my mistress, that you were so tiny when Joe brought you home that he carried you in his coat pocket. He handed you in the palm of his hand to her. You must have been darling!

My name is Wags. I am brown and white, have short hair and am seven years old. What a lot of fun and what interesting experiences I have had in those seven years!

We are most eager to see you. Do come to visit us soon.

Bye!   Wags

Who's Training Whom?

Five-month-old Holly decided she'd teach her struggling parents a lesson in dog training. Every time they left her by herself in the kitchen, she entertained herself by shredding paper...usually the newspaper. They would return to a kitchen floor covered in "confetti."

They tried moving the newspaper to "higher ground," namely the kitchen island. However, the new location merely inspired higher jumping on Holly's part. One day, Holly's mother came in and found a different kind of confetti on the floor. Aghast, she noticed Holly had shredded a hardback book. Totally exasperated, she turned to her husband and said, "She's *your* dog. You take care of this."

A few minutes later, he walked out of the kitchen, laughing. "You know that book Holly shredded? It's the one I borrowed — *How to Train Your Bird Dog*."

The family dog always knows how to find the best seat in the house.

Love Me, Love My Dog

Try This...

Make a quick list of all the pets you've loved. Opposite each name, jot down the first words that come to mind. You have just started your collection of animal anecdotes.

_____

_____

_____

_____

_____

_____

_____

_____

_____

_____

_____

_____

_____

_____

_____

_____

_____

_____

_____

_____

_____

COSTUMES

Costumes trigger laughs, fantasy, fun, and special memories. Through the years, theme parties and Halloween costumes have been ongoing favorites for all ages. In addition, the neighborhood show is as timeless as the lemonade stand. So are school productions. Attics, closets and dress-up boxes still inspire creative, side-splitting times with family and friends.

Superheroes and celebrities are a natural fascination for children. They also inspire party themes, costumes and imaginative play. Young parents, get ready for the fun you can have watching, photographing and chronicling your child's various identities. Keep your cameras loaded and a pen at hand.

The Lone Star

"As soon as I got the letter asking for a childhood picture to surprise my daughter, I knew which one I'd send," said a Texas mom. "My obvious choice?…a picture of a 5-year-old dressed in a red cowgirl outfit, boots, hat, and all. I understand the crowd went wild with laughter when the picture appeared on the screen. After all, she was the only Texan in her sorority."

Grown-up Dress-up

"I still love to dress up for Halloween," says Lynlee Linke, mother of twins. "That's why Joe and I have such fun hosting our annual Halloween Party. The first year, we dressed as Cleopatra and Mark Antony. When I was pregnant with the twins, I dressed up as the Prize Cow, and Joe donned a Farmer Brown costume. I am already thinking about how we'll dress for the next party."

COSTUMES

Ideas!

Choose among the following to create your Family "Costume" Originals.

1. Do you remember donning a cape and becoming Superman or sprinkling glitter as Tinkerbell? Did you win the West as a cowgirl or cowboy? Did you scale the heights of Gotham City or work the wonders of Captain Marvel? Recapture the magic of those characters in an album.

2. Although adults often act like children, children rarely get to act like adults. The dress-up birthday party is an exception. If you have a classic picture from one of these parties, consider using it as part of the party invitation when one of "the ladies" has an adult milestone birthday. If you are computer savvy, you can scan the photograph yourself to make your invitation; otherwise, consult a local printer or copy shop.

3. Don't masque your memories. In fact, showcase them in a collage. Collect pictures of your spooks and goblins, your lions and tigers, your princesses and little mermaids. Think of all the family fun you can have revisiting Halloweens past. If you prefer, have someone else make the collage and surprise your family with it. There are resources on the Web you can find by typing "personal photo collage" into any search engine.

4. What about holidays other than Halloween? For example, if you or your children ever participated in the Christmas pageant, surely there is a photograph. Since there can only be one Mary and one Joseph, somebody has to be the sheep. Was it you?

5. Who are your family stars? What shows are in your family repertoire...including backyard and in-house productions...and, of course, the more elaborate dance recitals? Don't forget school plays, puppet shows and church programs. Were you or your children members of the chorus, band or drama club? All of these suggest "costumes" and can easily be included in an album or collage around this theme.

6. "Play around" with possibilities. You can create an album or collage around one family member in various roles. Entitle this one "Starring Roles." You can also put all the family characters in one album or collage. A fun title for this version is "Family Characters through the Years."

Fun, flavor and imagination are part of the dress-up scene, regardless of your age.

Costumes at Christmas

There were no "chestnuts roasting on an open fire" the Christmas Eve Aimee Ford's family went bowling. One group in tinsel wigs and the other in clown wigs signaled "just another one of 'Aimee's Holiday Tradition' parties." said Aimee's mother, Jaunea Ford.

Jaunea says the party and dress-up idea evolved when "Aimee became gainfully employed and poor at the same time. She decided she would plan a surprise family event each holiday as her gift to her family. She worked this out well," says Jaunea, "because I still get to cover the cost of food and drink while Aimee just works on the creative party idea and the costumes.

"One Christmas we had a Karaoke party with a 9' po' boy dinner. Another we made pottery, while yet another was a family paintball competition. Always involved is a costume or some sort of wig or hat to differentiate teams. Our family loves gathering for Aimee's crazy and fun holiday events."

Add an element of fun at your next holiday gathering by getting your family to "change hats" for an activity. Be sure to have your camera handy.

Helpful Tips for Young Parents

1. Anticipate, anticipate, anticipate. Most of us have the camera on hand for birthdays and Halloween. Sometimes, however, it's the unexpected moments that tell the best stories. Therefore, keep your camera loaded, and a pen and tablet at hand. Snap a picture of your child dressed up for a birthday party, a recital, a backyard show, or just plain playtime.

2. For developed pictures, keep the best, throw away the rest, and identify names, dates and occasions on the back.

3. Save programs from school and religious productions. They are records of your children's performances. You can match them with corresponding pictures in an album.

COSTUMES

Even Superman came

What could be more fun than spending a warm afternoon sitting in the middle of a cake walk at a school festival in your Superman suit, reading a comic book and drinking a Coke? Walt Barron, 3, can't think of a thing he'd rather do. He's the son of the Rev. and Mrs. W.R. Barron of Marianna. His mother, Eleanor, was in charge of the cake walk at the Golson Elementary School "Spring Festival" Thursday, which raised approximately $300.

"When I was young, I didn't just dress in a Superman costume at Halloween," says Walt Barron. "I *was* Superman and dressed the part as often as my mother would let me out of the house in my suit and cape. One day a photographer from the local paper passed by and saw me, Superman, on the sidewalk. He snapped this photo, which is living proof that I had a super childhood."

An Elvis Sighting on Gilligan's Island

Well, not exactly. However, one supper club did incorporate Elvis Presley and the characters from the television show "Gilligan's Island" the year they decided to have "theme dinners." Rumor has it, some of the members of the club had to catch the re-runs to reacquaint themselves with the castaways. It worked. The crowd came in character and enjoyed island décor and fare. Not a soul felt stranded, either.

Not to be outdone, another host couple chose Elvis Presley as the theme. The entrée that evening was "Chicken À La The King." One member went to the local bargain store and just happened to find a colorful beach towel featuring "The King" himself. This innovative woman turned that beach towel into a skirt and completed her rocking attire with a pair of blue suede shoes. She was definitely labeled the "best dressed" person at the table.

If you're in a supper club, tap your creativity with the theme idea. It's a great way to add a new twist to an established group. Remember the secret ingredient is your camera.

Try This...

Look around you to see how people add spark and flair to their dress even when "costumes" are not required. For example, how much red, white and blue do you see at a Fourth of July picnic? And at a football game, does one glance at the stands tell you whose fans are sitting where? When your clothes reflect your spirit, the fun is multiplied for everyone. List events you have coming up in your family that lend themselves to "dressing the part." It can be as simple as asking everyone to wear red for Valentine's Day.

The Great Pretenders—In Costume

"Since they loved to play dressup and pretend around the house, I signed them up with a local theatre company," Celia Leggett says of her two daughters. "They have had a fabulous time, and have also gained a lot of confidence.

"I never thought my life would have so many costumes in it," continues Celia. "In fact, costuming is where I come in (aside from all of the driving). Frequently the directors give the costuming assignments to us volunteer 'theatre moms.' Sometimes we piece costumes together, other times we find them at thrift stores or vintage clothing stores, and occasionally we just have to hire someone to make them.

"Challenging assignments have ranged from the flying monkeys in *The Wizard of Oz* to the swan in *The Ugly Duckling*. It always seems to come together, and the girls look adorable on stage. And what great photo opportunities for doting parents."

With programs, pictures and comments in albums, "theatre moms" can not only chronicle their children's lives on stage, but also create their Hollywood dossier.

PHOTO OP:
These high school students are "sharing the spotlight" with a celebrity and have the photograph as evidence.

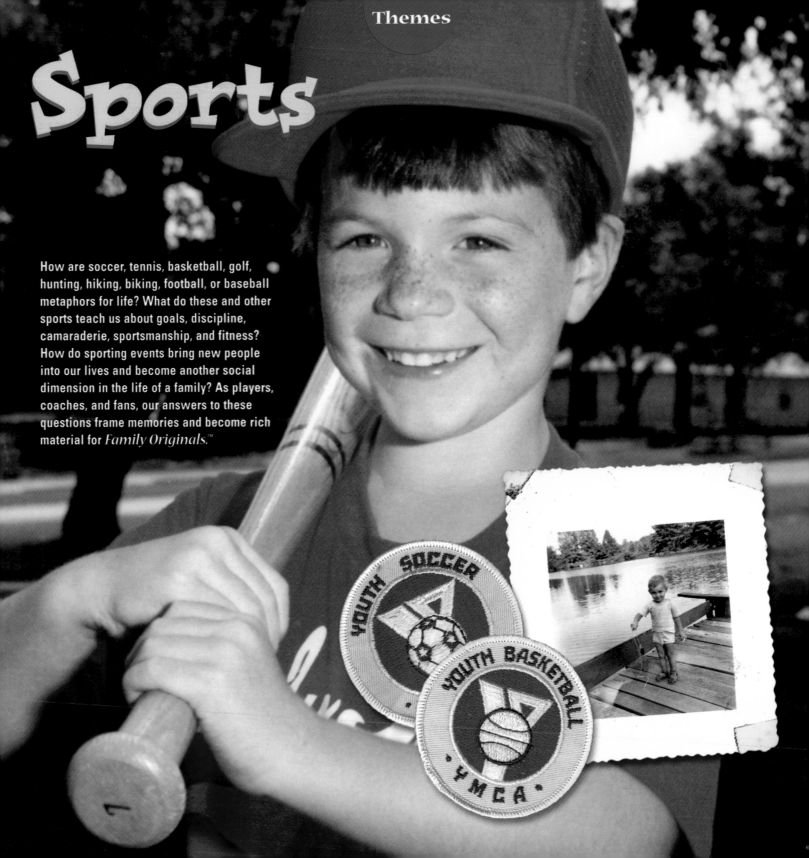

Sports

How are soccer, tennis, basketball, golf, hunting, hiking, biking, football, or baseball metaphors for life? What do these and other sports teach us about goals, discipline, camaraderie, sportsmanship, and fitness? How do sporting events bring new people into our lives and become another social dimension in the life of a family? As players, coaches, and fans, our answers to these questions frame memories and become rich material for *Family Originals.*™

My Championship Season

Today this scrapbook is the centerpiece of the coffee table in the family room. Even three years later, James (right) and his friend Richard Bunch turn the pages to relive a summer of glory.

At age 12, James Bristow became a star, and his mother Anne has preserved the story. "The year was 2001, and James had made the all-star team of the Palmetto Baseball League," she says. "It was a 'magical summer.' Those players just came together. They started winning…and winning…kept winning…and winning." Ultimately, the team went to the AAU (Amateur Athletic Union) National Championship, which happened to be in Minnesota that year.

Anne put together an album for James capturing this magical time. "The focus of the book appealed to me for several reasons," says Anne. "One, the story is fun to remember and captures something very positive. Second, it was a precise time period which gave the project focus and parameters. The album begins the day the boys were named all-stars and follows the tournaments in the state all the way through the National Championship. I enjoy the creative process, and this allowed me 'to create something that will last forever.'"

Anne continues, "The magic went beyond the camaraderie of the team and the parents. It became a story about families…the players' siblings and grandparents as well as parents. As I put the scrapbook together, I relished reflecting on how all those people came together and shared such a special chapter in family history."

This scrapbook is a mixture of photographs, programs, brochures of places they went in Minneapolis, ticket stubs, stories, and stats. A mother of four, Anne worked on this project in increments. "I would spread it out on the kitchen island those nights when I was waiting up for my teenagers to come home and was able to put it together two pages at a time.

"Putting together this book has made me approach subsequent events with a different eye. I plan to make a scrapbook for each of my children, and each one will have a different emphasis because my children have such different interests. The theme idea is a way to manage and focus on the project."

Sports

Ideas!

1. Leagues are legendary in an athlete's life. They also define chapters in a family's life. List the leagues you've participated in…as player, coach or fan…from little league and neighborhood leagues to church leagues. For each one, jot down memories. You can then record these stories in a journal or album. Supplement them with corresponding photographs, programs and any other memorabilia you might have.

There are resources galore. Start with your local Yellow Pages or any Web search engine, and look under "scrapbooks."

2. Young parents, here's an idea you can start now and keep repeating…a rolling record of sports in your child's life *and* in your family's life. Here's how you do it:
- Take pictures.
- As soon as they are developed, quickly identify people, events, dates.
- Purchase one calendar that has space for daily notes. Keep it handy to jot down "monumental moments" as they occur. You can go back to these "records" if you decide to put together an album or tape of memories.
- At the end of the season, record on video or audiotape impressions of family members…players, parents, grandparents, and friends. You can continue this chronicling through high school. When graduation comes, you automatically have an amazing gift: a set of tapes or albums of the sports history of your son or daughter.

3. Do you need an easy gift idea for someone who has influenced your love of a particular sport? Just purchase a memoir of a celebrity in that sport. For example, *Final Rounds* is a perfect gift for an influential golfer in your life. Write a note or inscription in the book about your meaningful connection. Keep a copy of your message for yourself.

4. Tailgating has almost become a sport in itself. Tap this social side of sports for *Family Originals.*™ Combine recipes and rituals in an album, collage, cookbook, videotape, or Web page. Entitle it "Story Tailing."

5. Certain places associated with sports have a mystical quality. That place might be a fishing hole, a hunting camp, a golf course, a lake, or a mountain retreat. A simple way to connect generations and that place is to create a collage of photographs of different generations in that setting. Label and date the photographs. Supplement them with any journal entries referencing that place. For additional ideas and materials, access "collages" on any Web search engine.

6. Interview older family members about ways a certain sport has affected their lives. Collect those stories in a journal or on tape.

7. Looking for a special gift for someone who has sports memorabilia? Collect those meaningful items such as autographed baseballs or signed jerseys or golf balls from courses played. Display these items together on bookshelves or possibly in a shadow box.

Another way to tell their story is in an album or a collage. Simply take photographs of the memorabilia and add the story behind these "signature items."

8. You don't have to have hiked the mountains of Colorado to create a *Family Original*™ around hiking. Make a list of your own adventures; then mark them on a map. Link memories and markers, and call your collection "Trails and Tales." Stories from the trail or around the campfire are as old as the West. What are yours?

9. Since many sports are seasonal, ranging from snow skiing to water skiing, organize your memories by the season. Who taught you to ski? Where did you go? What stories did you share at the end of the day? Who taught you to swim? Did you belong to any sports clubs or teams? Record these memories in a journal, in an album or on audiotape. For an easy gift idea for a sports person on your list, select 12 meaningful sports photographs and arrange them by season. Take them to a copy shop and have a calendar made.

Championship Meet

When Richard Barron became the women's basketball coach at Princeton, Maureen Daves, the women's softball coach, was assigned to show him around and welcome him to campus. Maureen impressed Richard so much he asked her to marry him and, a year later, on September 14, 2002, they became a team for life. The bride and groom scored extra points when both basketball and softball players showed up to cheer them on. This picture gives a clue as to which team is which.

Picture Party! Here's a great party idea: Get friends from your team together, share pictures, and make collages to capture a season. You can even include pictures of tailgating, fans and the pizza party after the game.

Sports

The picture-taking mother of this University of Texas football
player, Casey Ford, was standing in the perfect spot at the
perfect time. No *Sports Illustrated* photographer could have
done a better job of capturing the electricity in the air than
Jaunea Ford did this fall Saturday afternoon in Austin.

Lewis and Dork Expedition

You don't have to have hiked the Appalachian Trail or have climbed Kilimanjaro to create your own *Family Original*™ backpacking story. Just ask Eric Lewis and Steve Nelson who took these teenagers on a three-day hike into the wilderness. When the trip was still in the planning stages, Steve set up camp in his backyard, testing all his paraphernalia and waterproofing his tent and ground cloth. His wife Betsy started calling him a "dork" and then dubbed the hike "The Lewis and Dork Expedition."

As you can imagine, during the hike it began to rain, and yes, Steve was well-prepared. The real dork then became Lewis. His tent flooded as water came in from the bottom and the top.

Because Steve knew this expedition would produce stories that might even be denied, the well-prepared hiker took along not only his camera but also his hand-held tape recorder. When these hikers returned to civilization, Steve had his recordings transcribed, and the Lewis and Dork Expedition became immortalized in pictures and words on a Web site. Indeed, these stories entertain to this day.

Big Fish Little Fish

List five of your favorite sports, including spectator sports. Beside each one, note who introduced you to it. From there, think of specific memories linking those people and sports. This first step can lead to a collection of stories in a booklet or on tape.

Vacations

Themes

We've been honoring memories of summer vacation since childhood. Remember the annual essay on day one of school– "What I Did on My Summer Vacation"? Vacation memories have also been recorded in home movies…now videos and DVDs…and photographs. That means you have rich sources for *Family Originals*.™ From playing on the beach to skiing down the mountain, from touring historic places to visiting friends and relatives, families have bonded and generated special stories. It's time to preserve them.

Self-Addressed

While traveling, is it hard for you to find time to write in your travel journal? Once you're back home and develop your film, do you confuse the locations in your pictures? If so, take heart. Betsy Haas has developed a wonderful way to preserve vacation memories.

"When our family goes on vacation, each of us writes a post card every day and mails it home. Every post card captures a moment in time in the handwriting, picture on the front, the list of activities, and even the postage. When we get home, we have a stack of post cards chronicling our trip. I put these in an album, along with our pictures. Then the next year before leaving home, we look at the album and get excited about the vacation ahead."

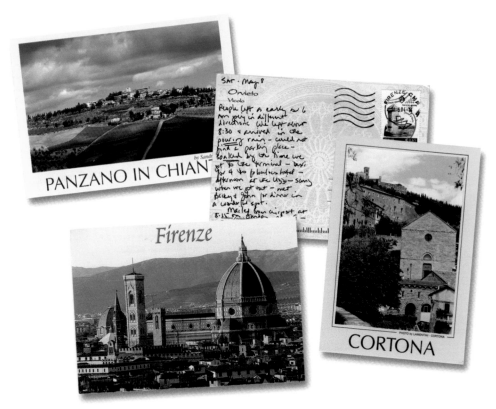

Vacations

Ideas!

1. For an easy gift that's fun and personal, select 12 vacation pictures for a calendar. Any copy or print shop can personalize your calendar. There are also calendar-making resources on the Web. Go to a search engine and type "personal photo calendars."

2. To entertain the family on long trips, create a set of audiotapes of vacation stories.

Here are some topics.

- "Unforgettable Vacations"
- "My Trip to Disney World"
- "Ski Trips"
- "Visiting Relatives"
- "Camp Memories"
- "Vacation Retreats"
- "Staying in Motels"
- "Staying in Campgrounds"
- "Visiting State and National Parks"
- "American History Vacations"
- "Disappointing Travels"
- "Visits to Theme Parks"
- "Family Reunions"
- "My First Cruise"
- "My First Flight"
- "My First Trip Out of the Country"
- "Spring Break"
- "Christmas Vacation"

Each one of these ideas can be expanded into an album. For example, with the camp idea, incorporate any letters your children wrote and the certificates they received. You might also include a list of expressions, inside jokes and copies of campfire songs.

3. Here's a great way to lasso all those vacation memories that have never made it to an album. Go through your pictures and group them by the places you've visited (Washington, DC or Uncle John's farm or YMCA camp). Then put a few of your favorites from each vacation in an album in alphabetical or chronological order. Include dates and highlights.

4. Collages are another way to chronicle vacations. You can focus on a particular trip or use favorite pictures from vacations taken through the years. You can use a print shop or a Web resource to create the collage. For information on Web resources, go to your favorite search engine and type "personal photo collages."

'Travels with Tutu'

"After a very long day in New York City visiting the Statue of Liberty, the Empire State Building, hiking through Central Park to the Metropolitan Museum of Art, my 7-year-old grandson, Hamer, and I collapsed in our bed," says Ann Muir. "He leaned over to me and said, 'Tutu, we really do make good traveling companions.' Tutu, by the way, is the Hawaiian word for grandmother.

"Once my grandchildren turn 6 years old, I take them on an annual trip," continues Ann. "These 'Travels with Tutu' have gone to places ranging from Seattle to New York, Hawaii to Italy. I plan the trips completely using the Internet and travel books, particularly those publications that promote kid-friendly hotels and restaurants. I also ask the kids if there are specific places they want to visit or things they want to do or see.

"The oldest is now a teenager, so on our last trip I suggested he might not want to travel with the younger children and me anymore. He commented, 'Tutu, as long as you are paying, I am going.' And I guess as long as the money holds out and my energy level is high, we will continue to have our 'Travels with Tutu' adventures."

Tutu's Tips

- Consider planning the first trip around visiting a relative so it will be less likely your grandchild will get homesick. You can visit the local sights.
- Before you go, have children read travel books to give you ideas about things to do.
- When visiting a museum, let everyone choose two or three exhibits to see; if time allows, you can see more.
- Use public transportation, subways and buses, as much as you can. There are adventures in that mode of travel.
- Have medical power of attorney when traveling.
- Buy a phone card so children can call home.
- Give each child a disposable camera to record the trip.
- Before the trip, find children's books at the library and local bookstores about subjects or places you will visit.
- Give children travel responsibilities; for example, plan the subway route from point A to point B.
- Have children write in a journal about the trip; younger ones can draw pictures about experiences.

Vacations

"Wake up, Dad! Mom's on the 'Today' show."

"I have started my morning with Katie Couric and Matt Lauer ever since they joined the set of the 'Today' show. That's why I was determined to appear on television when we went to the Big Apple for a family wedding," says the 'Today' show fan Lucy Lewis.

"The rest of my family did not endorse the idea, so at 6:00 AM I tiptoed out of the hotel leaving my sleeping loved ones behind. As I charged toward Rockefeller Center, I heard a familiar voice behind me, 'Hey, Lucy, wait up!' The voice belonged to my nephew James who knew of my plan to visit the 'Today' show and wanted to get in on the act."

As Lucy and James stood behind the NBC barricade, Lucy held up her sign which simply stated, "Today is my 30th Wedding Anniversary." It worked. Al Roker approached Lucy uttering the words, "This lady is having a 30th wedding anniversary today." He then asked Lucy her name and hometown. By this time, James was edging closer to the camera to share the 30 seconds of fame. Having a lot of fun, Al asks, "Is this your husband?" referring to 13-year-old James. When Lucy clarified that James was her nephew, Al asked the follow-up question: "Well then, where *is* your husband if this is your anniversary?"

Lucy meekly answered, "He's back at the hotel sleeping."

Al responded, "Well, I guess that is why you have been married for 30 years."

Meanwhile, back at the hotel, Lucy's daughters had turned on the television in the nick of time to scream, "Wake up, Dad! Mom's on the 'Today' show."

Year-Long Vacations

"I love to take pictures of my family on vacation," says Susan Dabbs, "but I always withhold 12 of my favorite pictures. My family gets to see those on Christmas morning when they find their Kinko's® calendar in their stockings. Now that my children have grown up, I'm collecting and combining 15 years of Kinko's® calendars in a book that recalls our vacations through the years."

Try This...

Think about your last vacation, and write down the first five memories that come to mind. If you have pictures that correspond, you have just started preserving family stories.

_____
_____
_____
_____
_____
_____
_____
_____
_____
_____
_____
_____
_____
_____
_____
_____
_____
_____
_____
_____
_____
_____
_____
_____
_____
_____
_____

Swinging Grandparents

When each of these children turned 13, they were treated to a "coming of age" trip by their swinging grandparents, Gerry and Jimmy Skardon. To make the adventure even more special, each child got to choose the destination. The oldest one chose New York City and, one by one, so did the other six.

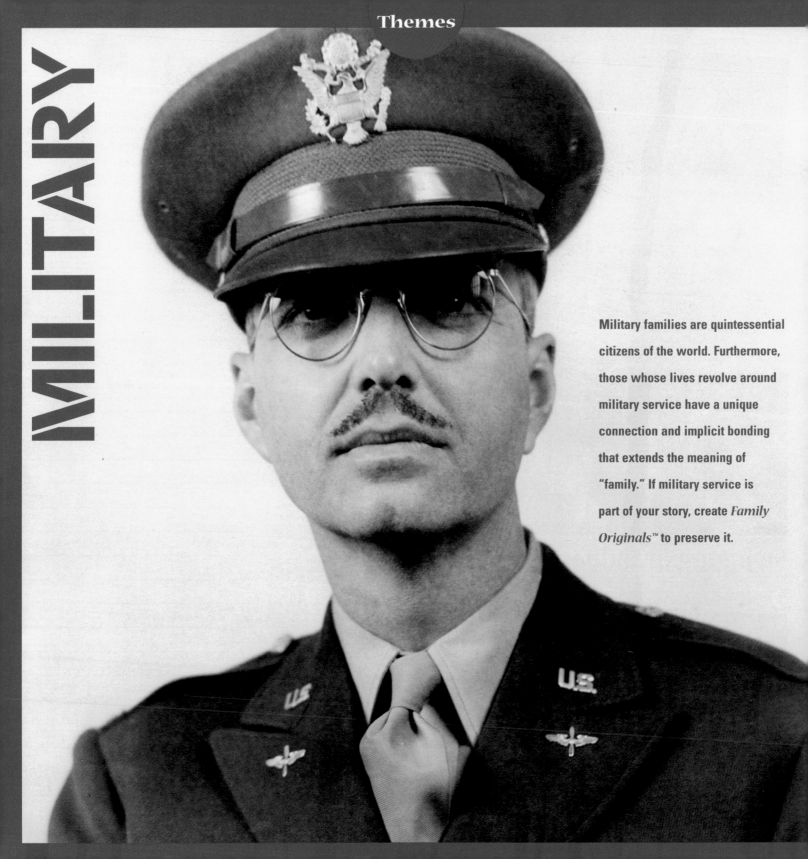

MILITARY

Military families are quintessential citizens of the world. Furthermore, those whose lives revolve around military service have a unique connection and implicit bonding that extends the meaning of "family." If military service is part of your story, create *Family Originals*™ to preserve it.

Great, Great Grandfather and the Civil War

Union Soldier Lt. Col. Newton T. Colby survived the Civil War conflict and so did many of his letters. Lt. Col. Colby's great, great granddaughter, Ann Cavanaugh, has a number of these letters which have been compiled with others owned by family members into a book, *The Civil War Letters of Newton Colby*. The entire collection of letters tells of battles, of life during conflict and even of the assassination of President Abraham Lincoln. A Union officer, Lt. Col. Colby served as a bodyguard at Lincoln's funeral, and wrote one letter describing his personal feelings and the mood of the country during that historic time. Ann has framed a copy of this particular letter along with a portrait of Lincoln as a very special gift for her son-in-law, who is an amateur Civil War historian.

MILITARY

Ideas!

1. Make an album about the different places you have lived. You could entitle the collection "Base Lines," "Touching Base" or "Bases Covered." Include pages from address books, addresses on envelopes, base photographs, and key moments in family history. A nice touch would be to add newspaper clippings that chronicle what was going on in the world at the time of your service.

2. Frame military insignia or medals.

3. Wartime correspondence and journals from both fronts, the home front and the battlefield, are a fascinating way to capture family and national history. With current military conflict, the correspondence could be e-mails. Create a *Family Original*™ collection of wartime correspondence. For a gift, duplicate the collection for family members.

4. Here's an interesting way to link the personal with the historical. Select excerpts from personal correspondence to combine with articles and clippings. Put your combination in an album or booklet to show how real lives intersect with historical events.

The English Patient

"I thought my job would be driving a truck for the military since I had had no combat training," wrote Paul Newton Whitt to his sister Callie while recuperating in an English hospital in 1944. "Fortunately, I grew up a country boy and had learned how to shoot, since I was quickly sent to the front lines," continued the 24-year-old soldier.

The letter tells Paul's story of lying on his stomach behind a hedgerow and engaging the Germans in battle when German soldiers snuck up behind and shot everyone in his unit. Paul, though wounded, was the only one in his group to survive the German attack.

Paul's daughter Samantha Sullivan now has the letter. She cherishes the connection to her father and the example of his courage which she can share with her children.

Years later as Whitt lay dying, this recipient of the Purple Heart asked for pen and paper. He said, "There is so much more that I would like to write down about our family and my own life and my hopes for you, my children." Because he was not well enough to write down everything he wanted to say, his family is very much aware of how powerful it is to preserve personal history while there is still time.

Vietnam Experiences

"I experienced the Vietnam War as a wife, daughter and mother," reflects Ann Muir. "My husband, Jimmy Muir, and my father, Frank Linnell, now deceased, were there at the same time in 1968. I worried very little about them; I was so young I didn't dwell on the dangers of war. When I was an Army daughter and my father was away on a 'hardship' tour, life was easier for me because the family disciplinarian wasn't home. As a young wife and mother, however, it was different; the risk was greater. Now that I reflect on it, my mother must have been very anxious, but she always put on a good front. However, she and I knew they were well-trained and my dad was certainly experienced. I also knew they were doing their job to support their commander-in-chief; they were there to keep their men safe and to seek out and destroy the enemy.

"My dad was a Brigadier General and was the commander of the 196th Infantry Brigade; he also served as the Deputy Chief of Staff Operations for USARV. Jimmy was an Infantry company commander in the 9th Infantry Division and, after being wounded and evacuated to Hawaii for nine weeks, he returned to Vietnam to be a protocol officer and then aide-de-camp.

"The war was not my husband's first time in Vietnam. As a teenager in 1957, he lived in Saigon where his dad was advisor to the Minister of Defense and also a temporary interpreter for the President of South Vietnam. His second time was his first tour of duty during the war in 1966, and that was with the 25th Infantry Division as a platoon leader and company commander. I stayed at home with my parents at Ft. Bragg, North Carolina with our newborn daughter. When he served his second tour, I didn't live with my parents since my dad was in Vietnam also, and my mother had enough challenges with my teenaged brother. We'd had a second daughter by then and I decided to live that year in Hawaii. As luck(?) would have it, Jimmy spent his recovery in 1968 with us.

"In 1966 and 1968, we didn't have e-mail, and we certainly didn't phone back and forth from Vietnam to the U.S. Our family developed a unique way to keep in touch with Jimmy. His parents would tape a message on a cassette tape and send it to me. Then I would tape on it after listening to their message and mail it to Jimmy. He would tape a message to his parents, and they would tape again and send it on to me. We had a Vietnam communication round-robin. We also wrote letters, and I saved all his letters. However, when you knew you weren't going to talk to each other or see each other for a year, hearing each other's voice was very special.

"Jimmy has said numerous times how much he would like to return to Vietnam. He claims the country really does have the most beautiful beaches in the world."

Thoroughly Modern Military

"For the two years we were in Korea, the Internet was our lifeline to family and friends back home," says Gwen Diehl, wife of U.S. Army Lt. Col. David Diehl. "It gave me a brand new way to think about communication. Because we were in a foreign country, I shared day-to-day experiences with people who are important to me. Having returned stateside," continues Gwen, "I have discovered that we kept in touch much better while we were overseas.

"The most important news we have ever shared was the birth of our son, Justin, who was born in Korea. As a new mother, I was profoundly touched by another mother's story. While Sgt. Shannon Turner was serving in Korea, her own 18-month-old son was in the loving care of family members back in the States. She wanted her son to recognize her voice as well as her face when she returned. Her way to do this was to read him bedtime stories on videocam. She could also receive, in return, videos of her son's growth and development."

Modern technology has not only helped military men and women feel closer to home, but this technology has helped them permanently chronicle their lives and experiences for future generations.

Three young men from Upper Montclair recently reported to Naval

JERE D. EGGLESTON

centers for flight training. They are Jere D. Eggleston, 335 Upper Mountain Avenue; Joseph G. Hjelstrom, 16

WILLIAM W. REYNOLDS

Northview Avenue; and William W Reynolds Jr., 204 Fernwood Avenue. Eggleston was a member of the Class of 1941 at Montclair High School.

Navy Aviation Cadet Jere Duncan Eggleston, son of Mrs. Robert D. Eggleston, 335 Upper Mountain Avenue, Upper Montclair, has been transferred to the Naval Air Station at Pensacola after successful completion of the primary flight training at Squantum, Mass. After three months of advanced flight training as a Naval Aviator, Cadet Eggleston will pin on his wings as a ensign in the Naval Reserve, or second lieutenant in the Marine Corps Reserve.

Jere Duncan Eggleston, 21, of 335 Upper Mountain Avenue, Upper Montclair, won his Navy "wings of gold" and was commissioned a second lieutenant in the Marine Corps Reserve this week following completion of the prescribed flight training course at the Naval Air Training Center, Pensacola, Fla., the "Annapolis of the Air." Having been designated a naval aviator, Lieutenant Eggleston will go on active duty at one of the Navy's air operational

USMCAS, CHERRY POINT, N.C.
MEDICAL DEPARTMENT AVIATION TRAINING COMPLETED

Name _Eggleston, J.D_
Rank _2nd Lt_   Serial Number _033891_

Course	Date Completed	Officer's Sig.
Altitude Training	3-27-45	_Eugene F. Haly_
Night Vision		

Retain this card. A duplicate entry should be made in the health or service record or in the flight log book.

MILITARY

Fallen Hero

"The thing that helped me deal with my grief was a Web site to honor Nathan" said Dennis White, father of Lt. Nathan White. Lt. White was a Navy pilot who died after being shot down over Iraq on April 2, 2003. "Friends and fellow soldiers, neighbors and reporters, and just plain fellow Americans who had heard about Nathan began writing their stories, their remembrances of him and their condolences. People who did not even know him contributed to the Web site. You think you know your child, but I found out so much more. It was good therapy for me to discover who my son was from a different point of view. The Web site is an ongoing comfort to me and a legacy for Nathan's three children."

If you have ever been to Arlington Cemetery, you have experienced the profound impact of the endless rows of white crosses. All who knew Nathan, however, will look beyond the rows of American history to remember the story of this son, husband and father of three, who paid the ultimate price in the name of freedom.

Often we wonder what we can do to support our troops. The Web is one way to find options. Go to any search engine, and type in "support our troops."

Military Honor

For most of us, the word "military" connotes order, structure and chain of command. That's why "creative military honor" sounds like an oxymoron. It is also the very reason members of the Davis family were so touched by what happened at a family reunion. "I was deeply moved by what my son-in-law Jed did for my uncle," said Becky Davis Huber.

This uncle, the most decorated veteran in Sumter, South Carolina, served with General Patton in World War II. Jed Sorensen, a soldier himself, presented a special medallion from his unit to this outstanding veteran in front of all his family. This unusual gesture linked service to country in three generations.

"I love this picture of my mother and father taken shortly after their marriage in 1942," says Nancy Gent Serebrenik. "They had been married only 18 months when dad was sent to Europe with the 4th Infantry Division, and they spent the next 18 months apart. Then Dad returned to Texas to rejoin his bride."

This couple is representative of all military personnel who must leave their loved ones to serve their country during both war and peacetime.

Make a quick list of family members who have served our country, be it in the Revolutionary War, the Civil War, World War II, the Vietnam War, etc. Your family's story becomes part of a bigger national story.

_____

_____

_____

_____

_____

_____

_____

_____

_____

_____

_____

Faith

For many people, faith and family are tightly woven. From rituals in the home such as saying the blessing to services in places of worship, faith shapes and mirrors values, beliefs and hope. Faith practices also reflect contemporary culture. Today, youth groups go on mission trips to foreign countries. All generations work on Habitat houses and support blood drives and shelters. Youth and adults alike participate in sports teams and scout troops, choir practice and Bible study.

Religious milestones from baptisms to funerals frame our lives and bring families together. What are the stories that sustain your faith? Take time to record the firm foundation of your family story.

Faith of our Fathers

Sometimes a building can connect us to the "faith of our fathers." Elizabeth Cloud traces her history to a small church in Dalton, Georgia that her great, great grandfather founded. Through the years this church has inspired faith and connected generations. "I chose to have my daughter baptized in this old church where my mother and aunt were baptized," says Elizabeth. "I am especially thankful my mother, a Methodist minister, could administer the sacrament of baptism." This service brought together three generations in a place where six generations have worshiped.

What are the special houses of worship in your history?

The Good Samaritans

"In 1972, while on summer break, a friend and I went to Mexico after summer school ended," begins Lucie Eggleston. "The third day we were there, our car flipped down a mountain, and my friend Pat Muirhead was killed. I knew I had to get help, but I didn't even know where I was. I just started climbing that mountain until I reached the road. A Mexican on vacation stopped and picked me up. He spoke English and drove me to the nearest clinic in a town called Rio Verde. I never even learned his name.

"When we got to the clinic, the doctor not only treated my wounds; he also took me home where his compassionate family cared for me until I could travel. The mother-spoon fed me; the little girls gave me their room and then sat by my bed. I spoke no Spanish; they spoke no English. Their beautiful young neighbor did, though. She helped me make all the necessary calls back to the States.

"Three days later, the doctor's family drove me to a village near the scene of the accident to identify personal things that had been salvaged: cameras, guide books, travel journals, electric rollers. Everything was there, including credit cards, traveler's checks and identification. I later found out the villagers had held a Mass for Pat.

"When we got back to the doctor's house, a friend of my brother was waiting to take me to Mexico City so I could fly home. As I told each member of the doctor's family good-bye, the two youngest girls ran to their room and came back with their piggy banks. Even their parting gesture was a gift.

"In an experience like this, the most familiar words can take on extraordinary meaning: 'I was a stranger, and you took me in.' Beginning with the man on vacation whose name I don't even know…to the doctor and his family, the kindergarten teacher who spoke English, the villagers, and the friend of my brother…all were instruments of a loving God.

"Many have read the parable of 'The Good Samaritan.' I have lived it."

Ever Mindful

Learning to say the blessing is a rite of passage. When Melton Bristow, the youngest of four, was old enough to say the blessing, he gave the traditional words a new twist. Instead of saying: "...and make us ever mindful of the needs of others," he confidently prayed, "...and make us ever mindful of the need for covers."

Family stories like these are blessings in themselves. Be "ever mindful" of them.

Profit from the Prophets

Children's sermons are a priceless source of memorable family stories. One Sunday morning at Eastminster Presbyterian Church in Columbia, South Carolina, the children were asked: "Can anybody tell me what a prophet is?" The immediate response—"You mean like 'profit' in a business?" came from young Clint Barker. His question could not have been more appropriate. His father was a banker and his mother, an accountant.

Do you have favorite stories of children's sermons? Be sure to preserve them on tape or in writing.

TRUSTWORTHY LOYAL HELPFUL FRIENDLY COURTEOUS KIND OBEDIENT CHEERFUL THRIFTY BRAVE CLEAN REVERENT

BE PREPARED

Becoming an Eagle Scout is a tremendous accomplishment, not only for the Scout but often for the entire family. Robert Fairey stands with his proud parents and grandmother at his Court of Honor ceremony. The official mission of the Boy Scouts of America is to "prepare young people to make ethical and moral choices over their lifetime by instilling in them the values of the Scout Oath and Law." The scouting experience is a great topic for an album.

Scout Oath

On my honor I will do my best

To do my duty to God and my country

And to obey the Scout Law;

To help other people at all times;

To keep myself physically strong,

mentally awake, and morally straight.

137.

Faith

Ideas!

1. Attention New Parents. Write a letter to your child the day of his or her baptism and give it to your child at confirmation.

2. "**Make a Joyful Noise**" **on audiotape.** Gather around the piano and sing your favorite hymns.

3. Make a list of religious terms or favorite passages of scripture. Then record a memory in which the passage or the term came to life for you. You can put these thoughts in a journal or on audiotape. One format to follow is this: "I was introduced to this passage when…, but I came to understand its meaning when…"

4. Who are the main characters in your faith story? Make a list. For each person, record on paper or on tape the story of their influence. Then express your gratitude for the faith they have modeled by writing to them and retelling the stories.

5. Have you ever been on a mission trip? If so, did you take pictures and keep a journal? If you did, consider pairing excerpts from your journal with pictures in a collage or album.

6. Make a collage of your journey of faith, including items such as pictures and certificates. Remember you don't have to make the collage yourself. You can go to your favorite search engine on the Web and type in "personal collages" to find full-service resources as well as articles and instructions for making collages.

7. Have you read books or seen movies that made "faith statements" to you? Why not compile your own "recommended reading list" or collect meaningful excerpts in a journal or on audiotape?

Short-term mission trips like this one to Haiti have opened foreign mission travel to all generations and all professions. These experiences foster broader understanding, direct interaction and life-changing perspectives. By taking pictures and keeping a journal, travelers chronicle their faith journey in a foreign land.

"Who's Mama?"

Graveyards are a rich source of family history that link people, place and faith. On vacation one summer, Bill Barron wanted to show his children the grave of his beloved grandmother. As they walked along the rolling terrain of southwest Virginia on that peaceful summer afternoon, Bill stopped when he came to his grandmother's grave, turned to his children and said, "This is where Mama is buried."

Meg, age 12 at the time, said, "Who's Mama?"

"I was overcome," Bill says. "How could someone so integral to who I am be a stranger to my own children? I stopped right there and started telling Mama stories."

When Meg, now 34, recalls that afternoon, she always says, "It was the first time I ever saw Dad cry."

The stories of significant people in our lives are only one generation from extinction. That's why it's important to "stop now" and preserve them.

Practicing Your Faith

Katheryn Shaffer Ray sees parenting as a ministry. "Our young children have their own morning prayer that goes like this: Dear God, help us to do Your will every day, in every way, in everything we say. Likewise, for our bedtime ritual, the children go over their God Blesses and God Thank-yous for that day."

Katheryn, who teaches Ethics, New Testament and History of Christianity at Episcopal High School in Houston, sees her faith as the key to living: "Faith helps us deal with everyday life—even the frustrations of potty training."

FIVE LOAVES AND TWO FISHES
by John Horman

presented by the Children's Choirs of H.P.P.C.

Try This...

To begin chronicling your journey of faith, jot down your "first thoughts" about...

Sunday School

_____

Sermons and devotional messages

_____

Bible study

_____

Inspirational books

_____

Inter-faith studies

_____

Circle meetings

_____

Wednesday night programs

_____

Camps, conferences and workshops

_____

Religious music—hymns, spirituals, choirs

_____

Sunday School teachers

_____

Youth advisors

_____

Church leagues

_____

Scouts

_____

Travel

_____

FOURTH OF JULY

When it comes to classic American holidays, nothing can top the Fourth of July. Maybe you spend this holiday in a vacation setting, or maybe it's a gathering time at home to celebrate with parades, picnics and fireworks. Some hometown parades are more elaborate than others, with families decorating everything from tricycles to dogs, convertibles to baby buggies, and fire trucks to Sherman tanks. These celebrations provide rich memories to teach family values and instill American pride.

FOURTH OF JULY

Ideas!

1. Link this national celebration and your own history in a *Family Original*™. At your next Fourth of July gathering, brainstorm a list of family members who have served the nation through volunteer work, community organizations, military service, elected office, and professional life. You will quickly see how "the story of a family is the story of a nation." You will also create a personal version of American history.

2. Sponsor a Fourth of July Hat Contest for your family or neighborhood gathering. Photograph the participants and make an album or videotape of the guests and their creations.

3. Make your own neighborhood or family Fourth of July parade, and videotape the procession.

Don't Rain on My Parade

Diane Pryor tells a great story about her youngest sister who was born on the 4th of July. A significant day in their family history is the one when they finally had to tell her all the parades were *not* in her honor.

Aunt Jessie Saved the Story

It's not often that property on the National Register of Historic Places is still in the hands of the descendants of the original owner. This is the case, however, for the descendants of William Harris. Wink Harris gives all the credit to his beloved and amazing Aunt Jessie.

Along with the home, Aunt Jesse helped save the story of William Harris and his life during the 1800s. She documented the story because she wanted her children and grandchildren to understand their roots and be able to imagine living in the 19th century.

To further celebrate the Harris family's well-documented history, several family members compiled a recipe book called *Cookin' Cousins and Family Tales*. It also contains pictures, history and stories. A favorite story tells "how our grandfather, Virgil V. Harris, prevented a lynching near Good Hope in 1901."

This personal heritage leads Wink to understand his forefathers' way of life as well as that of most settlers in early America. Wink notes with pride that his relatives "in the 1800s were independent and resourceful. The acreage provided row crops, wheat and cotton. The family made their own soap, clothing, candles, and shoes. An herb garden, adjacent to the cabin, supplied medicines and herbs for cooking. Not far from the log house is a smokehouse for preserving meat."

This land can be traced to the Creek Indians who sold it to Walton County, Georgia, in 1818, and the family has maintained it ever since. Mrs. Jessie Harris did her family a great favor by preserving the Harris Homestead and its history, but she also gave the nation a gift by preserving a piece of American history during the early days of the state of Georgia.

What do you know about the land where your family settled? What about the resourcefulness of those who have gone before you? Ask members of "the greatest generation" about resourcefulness during the Great Depression, and then ask yourself what you are doing to preserve our precious natural resources today. How has the area where you live changed just during the time you have lived there, and how have those changes intersected with your own life? Answers to these questions should be recorded.

FOURTH OF JULY

The Box

"When I was a teenager," begins Carol O'Day, "I loved nothing more than visiting my Aunt Connie. She lived in Amish country and understood animals in an amazing way…sort of like a vet without a degree. She had goats, sheep, bunny rabbits, many that were sick, but Aunt Connie saved them. She hatched her own chickens, and once, when someone was selling peacock eggs, Aunt Connie bought some and raised peacocks in her back yard.

"The summer I turned 40, I started thinking about those special memories and realized I had not seen my Aunt Connie in years. I called her, and we picked right back up. My husband and I decided to stop by to see her while we were on vacation in Pennsylvania. Little did I know what awaited me."

Ewertz, Eric	August 31, 1893	Liverpool & Queenstown

Built by J. & G. Thomson Limited, Glasgow, Scotland, 1878. 4,809 gross tons; 430 (bp) feet long; 44 feet wide. Compound engine, single screw. Service speed 13 knots. 1,400 passengers (300 first class, 1,100 third class).

Built for Cunard Line, British flag, in 1878 and named **Gallia**. Liverpool-New York service. Chartered by Compania Transatlantica Line, Spanish flag, in 1896 and renamed **Don Alvaro Bazan**. Reverted to Cunard later in same year. Stranded in 1899; later salvaged. Scrapped in France in 1900.

Ellis Island Passenger Record

Name:	Ewertz, Eric
Ethnicity:	
Place of Residence:	
Date of Arrival:	August 31, 1893
Age on Arrival:	20y
Gender:	M
Marital Status:	
Ship of Travel:	Gallia
Port of Departure:	Liverpool, England, UK

During their visit, Aunt Connie showed Carol a box containing photographs and other memorabilia. The most amazing document, however, was her great grandfather's 125-page typed autobiography. Carol and her husband George left Aunt Connie's that day with evidence of a legacy she had not known was hers. The story of her great grandfather, Eric Ewertz, also opened up an America Carol and George had not fully grasped in any history class.

In 1893, without knowing a word of English, Eric Ewertz left his native Sweden and came to America. He became a successful engineer and later served his adopted country in World War I. In fact, the box contained a newspaper article stating Eric Ewertz was recommended to President Calvin Coolidge for a special commission to investigate a naval submarine disaster.

ASKS PRESIDENT TO PICK EWERTZ

Elizabethan Nominated to Probe S-4 Disaster.

Special to the Journal.

WASHINGTON, Jan. 21.—Eric H. Ewertz, of Elizabeth, was to-day suggested to President Coolidge for appointment as one of the members of the proposed commission to investigate the disaster to the S-4 if Congress adopts the resolution recommended by the President and the Secretary of the Navy.

The resolution providing for a commission of three civilians and three retired naval officers. The House passed the resolution ten days ago, but its adoption is being strenuously opposed in the Senate by the Democrats, who insist that a special committee of Congress conduct the inquiry.

Mr. Ewertz's name was presented to the President by Congressman Ernest R. Ackerman, of Plainfield, on recommendation of the Elizabeth Chamber of Commerce. Ewertz lives at 163 Westfield avenue, Elizabeth. He is a civilian, not a former naval officer. He is a practical shipbuilder of long experience, formerly with the old Crescent shipyard, later operated by the Bethlehem Shipbuilding Company. He was superintendent and general manager of the Elizabeth plant.

Carol continues, "I was also moved by a story he recounts about testifying in a trial. Today we would call him an 'expert witness.' Because of his testimony, the attorney won the case in what I like to think of as a 'Perry Mason moment.' Afterwards, the victorious attorney told my great grandfather, 'We'll give you anything you want,' and his response was not what the attorney expected: 'I want to call you by your first name.' That unassuming response showed me he was capable of being magnanimous, and that means I have choices, too."

Inspired by the autobiography, Carol researched her great grandfather's immigration records by going online to EllisIsland.org. She included the documents along with contents from the box in a bound collection. She then had the collection reproduced for family members. Her younger brother was so impressed he read it three times.

"When I left Aunt Connie's that day, I had no idea what I was going to do with that box. I was just so glad to reconnect with Aunt Connie. Once I started going through the box, though, I found myself on a journey of self-discovery. I became a detective in my own life. Here was all this history—my history, and it could have all disappeared."

What boxes of family history are waiting for you to discover? Since we are a nation of immigrants, how does your story reflect our nation's story? Become a detective in your own life and find out.

The Greatest Generation

"In the early summer of 1999, the news media buzzed with Y2K talk," remembers Mica Nixon. "Those of us who worked closely with residents of a retirement center in Clinton, South Carolina realized that they, indeed, were members of 'the greatest generation.' Collectively, these residents had experienced the entire span of the 20th century.

"To end the century on an optimistic note for them, we decided to plan a New Year's Eve celebration honoring their lives. To create a photographic display, we solicited pictures from them with the help of their families. We began to interview them about the pictures. As the narratives and the pictures came in, the story began to take on a life of its own, leading us to create a video presentation with narrative in the residents' own words.

"We came to understand how individual lives intersect the face of history. Evalina Kuehn's father was the first mate on the first ship to go through the Panama Canal when it opened. Burton White's father owned a mining business in North Carolina, mining mica for the old gas mantles. Sometime around 1910, Burton thought, Thomas Edison spent a week at her home while looking for cobalt for his electric light. Early during their marriage, Juanita Pitts' husband worked in the CCC (Civilian Conservation

Corps) camps for $1 a day. Helen Ballard's house payment in the 1940s for a newly constructed brick home was $17.28. Frances Martin remembers when women got the vote. Mary Junker's mother died in the flu epidemic of 1918. Lillian Brown remembered an ocean voyage when she was a bride, taken on a ship in which Amelia Earhart was also a passenger. Planes flew overhead and dropped red roses on deck for Amelia. Several folks attended the 1939 New York World's Fair. Addison Needham remembers and describes the end of World War I in New York City. Jeanette Jordan learned to pilot a plane as a part of a World War II women's flying group called 'powder puff pilots, the 99s.' Barbara Hollis was an Army nurse in England during World War II. Others experienced key battles and places during World War II.

"This labor-intensive process turned out in a way to be my salvation. As the summer was ending, my own mother was diagnosed with terminal cancer. My brothers and I scrambled to help her get her affairs in order and to find nursing assistance which would allow her to remain in her own home until she died. The ensuing weekends and sometimes weeks were spent in North Carolina. Time in Clinton was consumed with this project.

"The two predominant streams in my life continued to merge, and the video, the picture gallery and the personal connections which had gone into creating them were part of a great healing process in my own life. The event itself touched universal chords and was far and above the most successful pulling together of the human spirit which we have accomplished in my years with activities at Presbyterian Home."

List significant national events that have happened during your lifetime. For example, do you remember September 11, Pearl Harbor, Neil Armstrong's walk on the moon? This is the first step in linking our nation's story with your own.

_____
_____
_____
_____
_____
_____
_____
_____
_____
_____
_____
_____
_____
_____
_____
_____
_____
_____
_____
_____
_____
_____
_____

Easter

For many people, Easter means happy kitchen activities…from making bunny cakes and decorating cookies to smelling vinegar while dyeing Easter eggs. Easter morning brings sunrise services, new outfits and Easter baskets. On Easter afternoon families gather for a holiday meal and egg hunts. This sacred spring holiday provides rich material for *Family Originals.*™

The Sins of a Child are Forgiven

One Easter Sunday the new minister asked the children to come forward for the children's sermon. They marched to the front in their Easter best and gathered around him. The minister held a "magic slate" for all the children to see, and then asked them to tell him something they had done that they should not have done.

The answers flowed freely, and he recorded them on the slate as they came.

> "Talk back to my mama."
> "Play with my brother's toys when he's not home."
> "Forget to feed the cat."
> "Pick on Jimmy's little sister."

The slate was full; the minister was ready to make his point and lift the page of the slate and say, "Jesus died to take our sins away."

Before he could do that, however, a single voice clearly said, "Hey, Daddy, I've got one more." It was the voice of his 5-year-old son.

"What's that?" the minister asked.

"Look up girls' dresses?"

The congregation broke up. After a moment or two, the humbled minister said, "You are right. You should not do that." Then he looked at the congregation and confessed, "Obviously, this is not going exactly as I had planned."

What entertaining Easter stories can you tell? Make sure you record them.

Easter

Ideas!

1. **"In your Easter bonnet..." or without it,** be sure to catch your family in their Sunday best—in a photograph, that is.

2. **Here's an idea for next Easter.** Produce your own "Easter Parade of Memories" by recording your stories of egg hunts, Easter baskets, Easter outfits, and Easter "prizes" for finding the "Golden Egg." Involve every generation in the storytelling.

3. **Videotape egg hunts.**

4. **Host an inter-generational egg hunt.** First comes the traditional part where children hunt for eggs. Then the children hide eggs for the adults. Inside these eggs could be certificates for gifts ranging from mowing the lawn or walking the dog, to washing the car.

5. **Here's another holiday cookbook idea.** Chronicle memories of making and decorating Easter treats. Collect these in an album along with pictures and recipes.

6. **Adapt your traditional Easter dinner for a mobile society.** Even though your mother served leg of lamb, baked carrots and creamed onions in the dining room, you can organize a more informal afternoon picnic for family and friends. Let everyone bring something, and eat on paper plates decorated in Easter colors.

7. **Here's a simple, creative way to entertain and educate your family next Easter.** Buy a bag of plastic eggs, and treat them like giant fortune cookies. Instead of filling the eggs with fortunes, fill them with memory starters. Possible topics include favorite Easter outfits, favorite egg hunt story, favorite Easter food, favorite Easter basket. You *can* put all your eggs—plastic eggs, that is—in one basket. It can be your centerpiece and family members can open the eggs one at a time around the table. Let the stories begin.

We Are All in Debt

"Every Easter I am reminded of a story my father, N.G. Barron, a Chaplain in the Army in World War II, told in one of his weekly newspaper columns," says Lucie Eggleston. "It was originally published in March of 1968."

You've probably never heard of Pete Kassos. Let me tell you about him. On August 9, 1942, I was aboard the Polish liner "Batory" in the north Atlantic Ocean. This proud ship had the distinction of being the "torpedo point" of the largest convoy that had ever left the United States in either World War I or World War II. It was a beautiful Sunday morning. There were ships as far as the eye could see, and we felt so secure as we noted the destroyers and battleships and airplane carriers that guarded us.

There was standing room only when I began the worship service in the mess hall, the largest room available aboard ship. When the service ended and we went out on the deck, there was not a ship in sight. We were on our own, for just as the service began, our ship left the convoy and headed north for Iceland while the other 120 ships went on to England. I have never felt lonelier than that moment when I could see nothing but water and sky.

Then we heard a plane. This lone plane was our escort and protection for the rest of our journey. In the summer there is no darkness in the land of the midnight sun, and so this lone defender had been flying day and night to shepherd our lone ship safely into the harbor. Then, when we were safely in the fjord where no submarine dare follow, he turned to go to the small airport a few miles away. The weariness of long hours had taken its toll, and we learned later that the plane crashed as it came in to the little landing strip and that Lt. Kassos was killed in the crash. I never knew him, but in a real sense he gave his life for me...

Think about that at Easter.

Try This...

Take three minutes and complete the following sentence:
Easter is...
This list will give you a "jump start" toward your own "Easter Parade of Memories."

_____
_____
_____
_____
_____
_____
_____
_____
_____
_____
_____
_____
_____
_____
_____
_____
_____

THANKSGIVING

Thanksgiving, a holiday that connects us to our national history, reminds us of the blessing of family. Whether you cook at home, go "over the river and through the woods to Grandmother's house" or go out for Thanksgiving dinner, it is a time to gather with loved ones in gratitude. Maybe that's why the older we get, the more we appreciate this holiday.

American Turkey, South American Style

Proud to call herself a first-generation American, Martha Alvarez has chronicled her Thanksgiving memories with their international flair in her photo albums. "Because my family does not have an extended family in the States, we have 'made our own' by getting together with six other families from Colombia. Even though we always have turkey," Martha proclaims, "it's usually a little different from the American version."

Martha tells the story of one over-zealous hostess who decided to add a creative "south of the border appearance" to the traditional bird. "She painted the turkey with food coloring before cooking so that it came out a bright yellow. On the buffet table, she decorated the turkey with grapes stuck on toothpicks. When the time came to carve it, she had to cut it into chunks instead of slices in order to work around those grapes and to preserve the decorative presentation." Martha laughs at this picture today, but adds, "It still tasted good."

What Thanksgiving stories can your turkeys tell? Why not record those memories this Thanksgiving when your family gathers?

THANKSGIVING

Ideas!

1. Here's a simple idea you can start this Thanksgiving and turn into an automatic tradition. Go around the table, and ask each family member or friend to fill in the blank: "This Thanksgiving, I am thankful for_____." It would be nice to record the list of blessings, date it and pair it with pictures from the holiday. Each Thanksgiving you can repeat these moments of gratitude and read lists from previous Thanksgivings. Think of the recorded history of blessings you will have to comfort and inspire your family in the future.

2. Interview family members, and record their memories of past Thanksgivings.

3. Collect favorite Thanksgiving recipes, and note the stories they evoke. Supplement with pictures of Thanksgiving celebrations throughout the years.

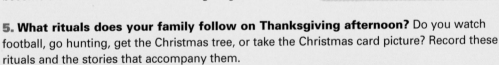

Sweet Potato Casserole

2 large cans yams, drained & mashed
1 stick butter melted
½ C sugar (you can add a little more)
2 t. vanilla
Mix well ; put in greased casserole.
Add topping :
1 C light brown sugar
½ C all-purpose flour
1 C chopped pecans   Bon Appetit !

4. Record how Thanksgiving has changed over the years in your family.
For example, the Flowers family now fries the traditional bird instead of roasting it. "Four Men and a Fryer" have become a social ritual in their Thanksgiving celebration.

5. What rituals does your family follow on Thanksgiving afternoon? Do you watch football, go hunting, get the Christmas tree, or take the Christmas card picture? Record these rituals and the stories that accompany them.

This Thanksgiving, Help A Child At Thornwell

The Cardboard Turkey

Our ordinary lives contain extraordinary moments. One such moment happened in 1960, at a small liberal arts college in North Carolina. On the Monday before Thanksgiving, freshmen in a required English class were asked to write a one-page essay on a Thanksgiving memory from childhood. One freshman wrote about a cardboard turkey that stood on the breakfast room table in his home in Alabama throughout the month of November. The turkey had 30 slots, and each day he filled a slot with a dime for the children at Thornwell, a home in Clinton, South Carolina, 350 miles away. In his essay, this college freshman acknowledged that in retrospect, stuffing dimes in a cardboard turkey seemed a little corny.

He handed in his essay and went home for the holidays.

The following Monday in class, the English professor addressed two students by name: "Please stay after class for a few minutes." He then gave each one of them an essay—the other student's essay—and asked them to read silently.

One freshman read about the cardboard turkey on a table in Alabama. The other read about Thanksgiving morning at Thornwell Home in South Carolina, where countless turkeys filled with dimes were presented to the children, and they were told: "People you will never see or meet filled these turkeys because they care about you."

We all touch people in ways we will never know. Who are the people who have touched your life? Why not write them a note of gratitude this Thanksgiving?

Try This...

Make a quick list of all the places you've celebrated Thanksgiving. Next to each place, write names of people who shared the celebration. These notes will trigger your Thanksgiving memories, which you can easily record on audiotape.

_____
_____
_____
_____
_____
_____
_____
_____
_____
_____
_____
_____
_____
_____
_____
_____
_____
_____
_____
_____
_____

Christmas

To many people, the word "Christmas" means tradition. Some families always have a cedar tree; others, a spruce; some, an artificial. Some families journey into the country to cut their trees; others buy theirs from the same person every year. When you put up the tree and how you decorate it can become family rituals. So can the opening of the gifts. Regardless of how you celebrate, consider Christmas a great theme for *Family Originals.*™

Christmas

Ideas!

1. Collect holiday recipes and photographs in an album. Be sure to add their corresponding stories. If your family sends photo Christmas cards and letters, include those in your album. Display this album prominently as a historical Christmas decoration and add to it each year.

2. Searching for a gift idea you can repeat year after year? Give a yearly ornament. You can begin at any point, even a baby's first Christmas. Over the years you will have given a collection. Hand-made ornaments are precious heirlooms, and photographs personalize and record moments in time. You don't have to make your ornaments, though. You can purchase beautiful and meaningful ones, too. The Web lists numerous ideas and suppliers. Go to your favorite search engine, and type "Christmas tree ornaments" for a list of resources.

3. There are books on the market for recording your Christmas memories. Complete a Christmas traditions book for members of your family. You can also make the completion a family activity at a holiday gathering.

4. Make an audiotape of favorite Christmas memories. Tell the stories of your most memorable Christmas gifts. Classics include bicycles, roller skates, electric trains, favorite dolls, tea sets, cowboy outfits, board games, musical instruments, and video games.

5. Videotape all generations talking about the Christmases of their childhood. This would be a great activity to follow Christmas Eve supper.

6. If you are a poet or an artist, make a unique Christmas card with original verses and/or artwork. If you are computer savvy, you can copy it on the computer. You can also take the original to any print shop for duplication.

7. Here's one easy way to instantly record your family history. Collect in one book those holiday letters and pictorial cards you've sent through the years. In the years that follow, keep adding to your book. If you haven't sent letters and pictures during past holidays, begin this year.

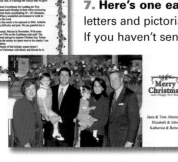

8. Here's an idea for next Christmas. Let music fill the air and the audiotape as you record your family singing favorite carols and songs of the season.

A Real Family Tree

Sometimes a civic volunteer project can lead to a *Family Original.*™ This is exactly what happened to Katherine Tutor when she started making ornaments for the "Trees of Christmas," an annual fundraising event that started more than 30 years ago in Meridian, Mississippi.

"Once I saw how much fun the ornaments were to make, I began making similar ones for my grandchildren. Each year the children would send several pictures, and I would select a couple and arrange them on ornaments. Then I would decorate around the pictures with braid, beads and beautiful trim. My grandson now has 31 very special ornaments, and his younger sister has 29."

These ornaments are a permanent record of the growth of the children, a testament to the love and generosity of their grandmother, and a *Family Original*™ for the next generation of family trees.

Ornaments connect past and present, but you don't have to make your own. You can consult your local craft and fabric shops for resources, or you can go to the Web. Just type "photo Christmas ornaments" in your favorite search engine to access a list of resources.

Tradition

Christmas traditions often span several generations. This is true at Sally Winfrey's on Christmas Eve. "We're a very traditional family," Sally says with pride. "I serve the same menu every year. In fact, it is so important that we do it the same way every year that I have taken pictures of each dish and its location on the buffet. I even have a Christmas Eve file which includes these pictures and each of my recipes."

The program that follows the meal is another dimension of the family gathering. In the beginning the grandfathers led the family service. Now the grandchildren serve in that role. The oldest reads the Christmas story from Luke; the middle child reads "'Twas the Night Before Christmas"; the youngest reads a scripture verse. Sally, who labels herself "anything but a real pianist," plays a few favorite carols, and the entire family joins in singing. This very traditional Christmas celebration captures a very traditional family.

Here's an idea for Sally's family and for yours, too. Videotape your family's Christmas Eve program. Family members may want to add favorite memories of past Christmases.

Ashes in the Eggnog

Often you can create an extraordinary gift by starting with a product on the market. This is what Angela Dina's mother did. She gave Angela a book she had purchased. The contents, however, were priceless. "Mama had filled in the pages with her wonderful memories, starting with Christmas as a little girl. The book continues with memories of Mama's youth, her first Christmas as a young wife and finally, Christmas as a doting parent."

Angela noted, "My own favorite pages have Mama's special Christmas cookie recipe and her stories of me as a child inviting a friend over to decorate the cookies with lots of colored icing."

Another favorite story relates to Angela's grandparents' party tradition. "They had friends over for eggnog every Christmas Eve. My grandfather always smoked his cigars a little too close to the eggnog, and there is a family joke that there were probably ashes in the eggnog. The thought still makes me laugh!"

What Christmas memories make you laugh? Record those stories now.

Christmas

Era of the Mushroom Soup Casserole

Aunt Missie knows your Christmas *Family Original*™ need not be something expensive or time consuming to touch a heart. The first year her nephew missed the Christmas gathering and his favorite asparagus casserole, Aunt Missie made a decision. "I just kept thinking about him and how much he loved that casserole, so I decided he had to have it. I boxed up a Pyrex® dish, a can of asparagus and a can of Campbell's® mushroom soup. I also included the recipe as well as an oven mitt, a can opener and a note saying,'You may have to miss the family gathering, but you don't have to miss the asparagus casserole.'"

That gift was a hit. "I knew I had touched a special chord in this young man's heart and stomach when he wrote me a thank-you note saying that this was the most thoughtful, fun and meaningful gift he had ever received."

Who on your list won't be home for Christmas this year? Why not package some of Christmas from home and send that special gift of connection?

The Stockings Were Hung

For over 30 years Mollie Merrick has touched the lives of close friends and family by knitting Christmas stockings for their children. For each of the 240+ stockings, she has followed the same pattern and included each recipient's name. "I have even numbered and recorded the name and date I knitted each stocking so that I can tell you what number your child's *Family Original*™ is. As the Christmas season approaches each year, I think of all these stockings I have made and celebrate the holidays with more than 240 friends and family members across the country."

If you enjoy needlework, why not share your talent and time with loved ones by making your gifts? These gifts from the heart and the hand are lasting connections with those we love.

Merry Christmas and
Godly Blessings
to you in 2004

Brooks was married in a family wedding in May to Kimberly Mills.
Sharita's passion continues to be saving the planet.
Jess loves retirement.
Betty is traveling with Jess and is still loving fund raising.

Happy Holidays
The Tutors

Grand-Dolls on the Mantle

Every now and then someone comes up with a one-of-a-kind gift to tell the family story. Cricket Lewis made her "Best Christmas Present Ever" for her mother-in-law when she showcased Gammy's eight grandchildren in exquisite hand-made dolls. To create these dolls, she started with the oldest and followed the set in descending order. For Gammy, the collection captured her grandchildren as they were in 1984. Gammy kept the collection on the mantle in her bedroom for the rest of her life so she could see it every morning when she opened her eyes.

Cricket got the idea for the dolls the year she asked Gammy what she wanted for Christmas. Gammy said, "The best present I could ever have would be to have all my grandchildren together."

Cricket honored that wish with original dolls. You can remember grandparents in many ways, including a collection of photographs. The important point is to remember.

Look at the names on your Christmas list. Jot down one holiday memory you have of each person. For your gift this year, give the person the memory and, if possible, a corresponding photograph. This is something the entire family can adopt, and every year give and receive pages of precious memories from your own life.

_____
_____
_____
_____
_____
_____
_____
_____
_____
_____
_____
_____
_____
_____
_____
_____
_____
_____
_____
_____
_____
_____
_____
_____
_____

Ready Made

When her daughter Betty graduated from high school, Jane Cunningham collected special memories in a beautiful photo album with slots for 4 x 6" pictures. She wrote an original poem which she sent to Betty's friends. Along with her rhyming instructions, she included two pieces of acid-free paper cut in 4x6" sheets and a self-addressed stamped envelope. This idea led to a treasured collection of memories for Betty.

Jane showed us how to adapt her simple idea for other milestones and celebrations. We encourage you to use them. Take advantage of colorful products on the market, and have fun selecting the album, the paper and the computer fonts. You'll be able to create an extraordinary *Family Original*™ for any occasion.

Betty soon will graduate,
And she'll be off to Kansas State.
Because you mean so much to her,
Your memory bank we'd like to stir.
To guarantee you won't be stressed,
The enclosed stamped envelope's
self-addressed.
You'll find two cards for you to use
(And oh, we hope you won't refuse.)
On each please note a recollection
That we'll put in a bound collection.
A memory, photo, wish, or quote,
So she can ponder what you wrote
And always be with you connected
Through memories you have selected.

Ready Made

For a birthday…

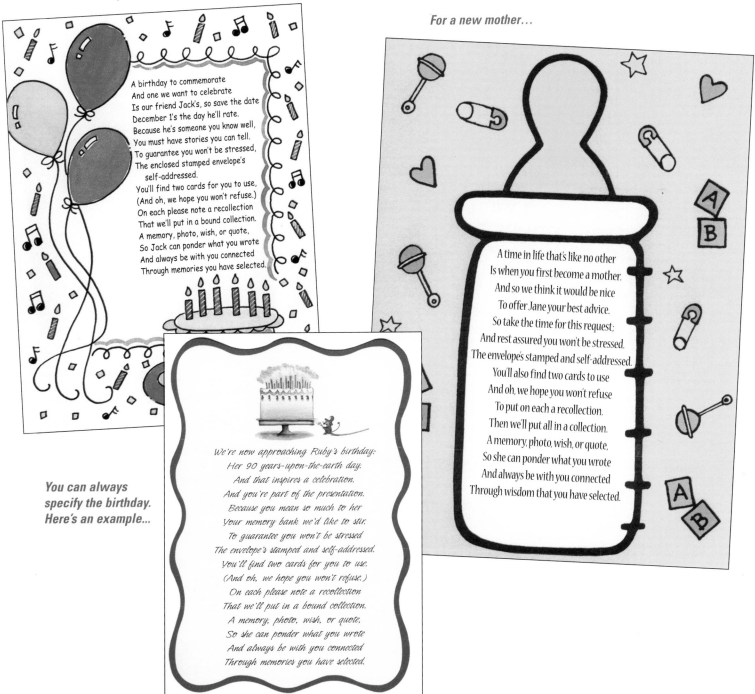

A birthday to commemorate
And one we want to celebrate
Is our friend Jack's, so save the date
December 1's the day he'll rate.
Because he's someone you know well,
You must have stories you can tell.
To guarantee you won't be stressed,
The enclosed stamped envelope's
    self-addressed.
You'll find two cards for you to use,
(And oh, we hope you won't refuse.)
On each please note a recollection
That we'll put in a bound collection.
A memory, photo, wish, or quote,
So Jack can ponder what you wrote
And always be with you connected
Through memories you have selected.

For a new mother…

A time in life that's like no other
Is when you first become a mother.
And so we think it would be nice
To offer Jane your best advice.
So take the time for this request;
And rest assured you won't be stressed.
The envelope's stamped and self-addressed.
You'll also find two cards to use
And oh, we hope you won't refuse
To put on each a recollection.
Then we'll put all in a collection.
A memory, photo, wish, or quote,
So she can ponder what you wrote
And always be with you connected
Through wisdom that you have selected.

You can always specify the birthday. Here's an example...

We're now approaching Ruby's birthday:
Her 90 years-upon-the-earth day.
And that inspires a celebration.
And you're part of the presentation.
Because you mean so much to her
Your memory bank we'd like to stir.
To guarantee you won't be stressed
The envelope's stamped and self-addressed.
You'll find two cards for you to use.
(And oh, we hope you won't refuse.)
On each please note a recollection
That we'll put in a bound collection.
A memory, photo, wish, or quote,
So she can ponder what you wrote
And always be with you connected
Through memories you have selected.

161.

Ready Made

For an anniversary…

Anniversary number 10!
(They say they'd do it all again.)
Join us all to celebrate;
July 14 will be the date
For Sally Martin and her mate.
Because you mean so much to them,
Think special thoughts of her and him.
Then send them, but you won't be stressed.
The envelope's stamped and self-addressed.
You'll find two cards for you to use.
(And oh, we hope you won't refuse.)
On each please note a recollection
That we'll put in a bound collection.
A memory, photo, wish, or quote,
So they can ponder what you wrote
And always be with you connected
Through memories you have selected.

or…

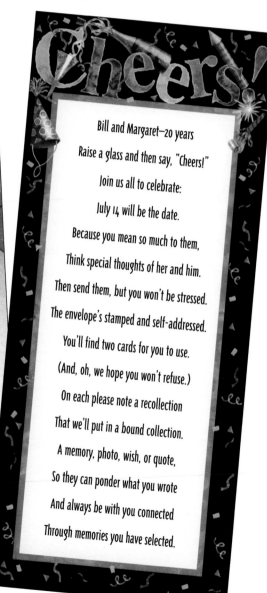

Bill and Margaret—20 years
Raise a glass and then say, "Cheers!"
Join us all to celebrate:
July 14 will be the date.
Because you mean so much to them,
Think special thoughts of her and him.
Then send them, but you won't be stressed.
The envelope's stamped and self-addressed.
You'll find two cards for you to use.
(And, oh, we hope you won't refuse.)
On each please note a recollection
That we'll put in a bound collection.
A memory, photo, wish, or quote,
So they can ponder what you wrote
And always be with you connected
Through memories you have selected.

For Father's Day…

As Father's Day is drawing nigh
Let's not let this one pass us by.
It seems a time to be reflective
And think of Dad from our perspective.
And so, my siblings, let us share,
Memories that say we care.
Take the time for this request;
Rest assured you won't be stressed.
The envelope's stamped and self-addressed.
You'll also find two cards to use
And oh, we hope you won't refuse
To put on each a recollection.
Then we'll put all in a collection.
A memory, photo, wish, or quote,
So he can ponder what you wrote
And always be with you connected
Through memories you have selected.

For Mother's Day…

Here's a day that's like no other,
For it's our chance to honor Mother.
And so, my siblings, let us share,
Memories that say we care.
Take the time for this request;
Rest assured you won't be stressed.
The envelope's stamped and self-addressed.
You'll also find two cards to use
And oh, we hope you won't refuse
To put on each a recollection.
Then we'll put all in a collection.
A memory, photo, wish, or quote,
So she can ponder what you wrote
And always be with you connected
Through memories you have selected.

Ready Made

For a wedding…

Andy and Karen will soon say, "I do."
To honor them now we need input from you.
Because you know them better than most,
Be thinking of stories to use in a toast.
To guarantee you won't be stressed,
The enclosed stamped envelope's self-addressed.
You'll find two cards for you to use.
(And oh, we hope you won't refuse.)
On each please note a recollection
That we'll put in a bound collection.
A memory, photo, wish, or quote,
So they can ponder what you wrote
And always be with you connected
Through memories you have selected.

For a promotion…

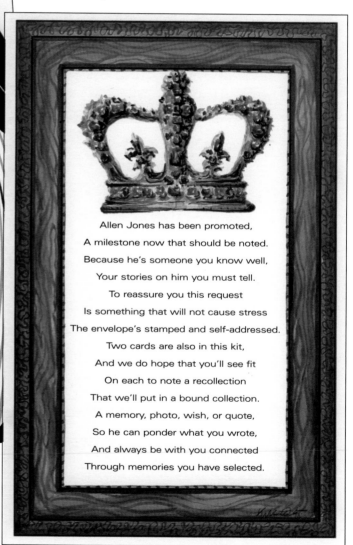

Allen Jones has been promoted,
A milestone now that should be noted.
Because he's someone you know well,
Your stories on him you must tell.
To reassure you this request
Is something that will not cause stress
The envelope's stamped and self-addressed.
Two cards are also in this kit,
And we do hope that you'll see fit
On each to note a recollection
That we'll put in a bound collection.
A memory, photo, wish, or quote,
So he can ponder what you wrote,
And always be with you connected
Through memories you have selected.

164.

Ready Made

For a retirement…

In May John Smith will be retiring

A goal to which he's been aspiring.

Because you mean so much to him,

Think now about this special friend.

To guarantee you won't be stressed,

The envelope's stamped and self-addressed.

You'll find two cards for you to use.

(And oh, we hope you won't refuse.)

On each please note a recollection

That we'll put in a bound collection.

A memory, photo, wish, or quote,

So he can ponder what you wrote

And always be with you connected

Through memories you have selected.

For a move…

The Johnson family will be leaving,

And that move is cause for grieving.

Even so we think it best

To send them off with fun and zest.

So while the movers pack with care,

A get-together we will share.

For you we have this small request

But guarantee you won't be stressed—

The envelope's stamped and self-addressed.

You'll also find two cards to use

And oh we hope you won't refuse

To put on each a recollection

Then we'll put all in a collection.

A memory, photo, wish, or quote,

So they can ponder what you wrote

And always be with you connected

Through memories you have selected.

For someone in assisted living…

Grandma's in assisted living,

But our love we can all be giving

Sending Christmas (birthday) thoughts and prayers

So she knows that each one cares.

So take the time for this request;

And rest assured you won't be stressed.

The envelope's stamped and self-addressed.

You'll also find two cards to use.

And oh, we hope you won't refuse

To put on each a recollection.

Then we'll put all in a collection.

A memory, photo, wish, or quote,

So she can ponder what you wrote

And always be with you connected

Through memories you have selected.

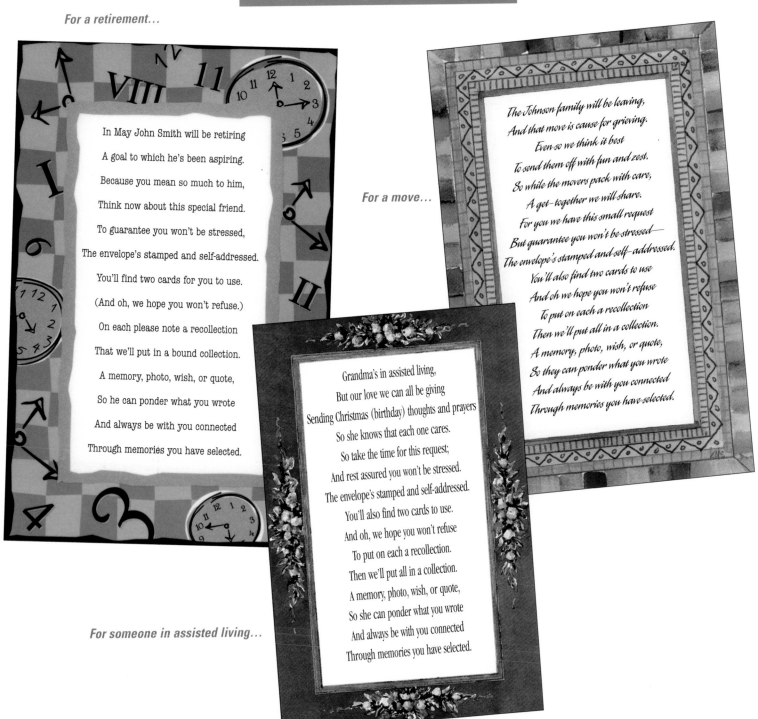

165.

Reality Check

If you are a new spouse or parent, for example, you have brand new, non-stop demands on your time. Yet, you're in a wonderful new chapter in your life, so you want to preserve the special, fleeting moments as they unfold.

If you are a baby boomer, you realize how quickly time passes. Yours is the generation that changed how "old" ages 30, 40, 50, and now 60 are. Your ever-youthful generation also knows the pain of loss and the reality that once someone is gone, you can't get that person back. If you are fortunate enough to still have members of the older generation in your midst, you understand the urgency of recording their stories in their own voices.

If you are a member of "the greatest generation," you are the *only* ones who can pass along the stories of the generations who came before you. You are their last best chance for speaking to those who have followed them. You know their words of wisdom, coping mechanisms and humor. Now is the time to articulate your lessons of a lifetime and theirs. Savor this time to reflect and recount the times that have preceded it. Share your stories to share yourself with those you love.

Each generation faces unique challenges in preserving the family story. We have found the following principles helpful. For all of them, *where you are now* is the starting point.

For New Couples and Parents

Adopt a few simple habits. Look ahead for special occasions coming up, and get ready in advance. Have your camera loaded. When you get your pictures, note on the back the occasion, people and date.

Your refrigerator may already record your family history with pictures, artwork and invitations. Transfer these to an album at the end of the year or, even easier, a photo or an archival box. You can also add your reflections to record your history as it unfolds.

On your children's birthdays, write an annual letter. Mention something special about them at this point in life, and add your hopes for their future. This annual letter can lead to a collection to present to your child at a later milestone in life.

Buy a spontaneity calendar or datebook with space for writing notes each day. This does not mean you will write in it daily. It simply means you'll have a place to jot down notes of highlights and priceless comments as they happen. There is no set number. You are not "scheduling" time each week to write in your calendar, but how many times have you heard someone say, "I wish I'd written that down"? With your calendar or datebook, you'll have a place at hand.

As a gift idea, give a datebook to a friend, and inscribe this idea in it. At the end of the year, they will have their own volume of family history.

Have a designated container for memorabilia about specific members of your family. For example, you may want to save letters or cards you receive about your children. You may want to save artwork or essays. If you date these pieces of your children's lives as you receive them, you will have that documentation if you ever decide to create a *Family Original*™ with them. You may choose to simply give the memorabilia to each of your children on their 21st birthday, or you may want to select 13 items from the container on their 13th birthday. You have many possibilities, but the good thing is you will have done your research and basic organization throughout their lives.

Inspire your peer group to preserve their family stories as they are unfolding. If possible, get together with others during "Mother's Morning Out" to work on creative gifts that tell your family story. Possibly share and swap talents. For example, if one friend is an artist, offer your skills for organizing her project as a swap for your friend's skill in designing yours.

Make a list of family members in the older generation who are still living. Some may live in the same place you do. Some may still live where they did when you first knew them. Some may have moved into retirement homes. Make it a point to get in touch with them and, if possible, pay a visit. You may even want to take several days and travel to various places to record your family story. Take your list of questions, your orphan photographs other people may be able to identify, your tape recorder, and your own memories of that person.

If your parents are still living, plan a trip with them to their home place. This will be easier for some people than for others, depending on where you live and on where you'll need to travel. The trip might take several days, but think of how special that time with your parent(s) could be. Seize the opportunity that's available to you. Carry your camera, your tape recorder, your map. Record all you can, including your own reflections of the experience.

If you have brothers and sisters, you can share stories, photographs and reflections of the experience. You might consider planning a storytelling weekend for parents and siblings in the home town of your parents.

Check the calendar for upcoming birthdays or anniversaries, and involve other family members in planning a celebration. Let the "program" for the event be favorite stories/memories of the honoree. Record the stories and take plenty of photographs.

Use your talent to celebrate family. Is there something you've always wanted to do…but didn't have the time…like take an art class or a writing class? It's your turn to do just that. You will have an automatic support group pursuing your shared interest. You will tap and honor something deep within you that begs to be expressed. Then you can turn your hobby/interest/talent/passion into a means of celebrating the gift of family. You can write family stories or photograph family members or paint subjects your loved ones prize. Get in touch with your talents, and then share them with those people most precious to you.

Hints to Jump Start Your Project

Use time to motivate you. What family milestone is on the horizon—a graduation, special anniversary or birthday, possibly a wedding? That event is already on your calendar. Use it as your goal for completing a *Family Original.*™

When appropriate, use professional resources to make it happen. Today you have available resources for duplicating and restoring heritage documents. The telephone book, local libraries, book stores, and the Internet are great places to go for information and inspiration.

Embrace the tools of technology. The Internet offers information and resources on every facet of preserving your family stories. Type in your subjects in any search engine just the way you think of them. Here are some of the ones we've tried:
• heritage photographs   • preserving old letters   • family reunions   • videotaping   • album making   • family cook books.

Start with something recent and readily available such as your most recent photographs. Turn them into a quick gift such as a framed picture, a personalized calendar or a collage created from duplicate photos.

Turn your project into a chance to see friends. If you want to make a heritage album for a family reunion, sign up with a friend to attend regular workshops with a scrapbook professional who can help you finish the project. If you wish to needlepoint a stocking for a grandchild, sign up for a needlepoint class to help you stay on track.

Develop a signature item. For example, you might make original crossword puzzles as your signature *Family Original.*™ You might give an annual photo calendar or a spontaneity datebook. If you write poems, you'll like the way the preceding chapter shows you how to take a basic poem and adapt it for many life events.

Abandon perfection! If art imitates life, remember that life is not orderly. The spots on a recipe card or the smudges on a letter add authenticity.

Have a great time as you take time to create *Family Originals*™!

Index of Gift Ideas

Acknowledgements

Bob & Eric

Katherine Pearson, without whom this book would have never happened

Bob, whose fish, venison, doves and flexibility provided nourishment and support

Eric whose photography, technology and patience got us on line and kept us in line

Susan, Robin and Catherine, who relinquished instant access to their mother in
loving support of the project

Rhett Barker, who managed our finances and read our early drafts

David Hunt, who transformed our words into pictures

Missi McMorries and Gene McClure, who made us legal

Family and friends, who are the main characters in all our stories

"That great cloud of witnesses" that surrounds us and lives on in their stories and in ours

Contributors

Janis and Tom Abernathy
Martha Alvarez
Mary Anderson
Martha Armstrong
Cathy Arnold
Craig Augenstein
Carolyn and Bill Avery
Andrea and Sterling Bacon
Betsy and John Bacon
Josh Bacon
Sarah Bacon
Ottie Lee Baker
Rhett and Bill Barker
Clint Barker
Jake Barker
Alden Barron
Eleanor and Bill Barron
Jane and Jim Barron
Karen and Andy Barron
Katy and Walt Barron
Lane Barron
Lynn and Porter Barron
Margaret Barron
Maureen and Richard Barron
Rae Barron
Ruby Hutton Barron
Shea and Jay Barron
Sibylle and Hutton Barron
Sophie Barron
Carroll Belser and Sid Gauthreaux
Ritchie Belser
Monika and Scott Bennett
Debbie Berner
Bennett Beutel
Brad Beutel
Caroline Beutel
Whitney Beutel
Cecile Bishop
Bertie Bond
Sally Boone
Anne Bristow
James Bristow
Melton Bristow
Jackie Brittingham
Sarah and Frank Brown
Richard Bunch
Dana Burns
Aimee Ford Byrd
Kathleen Bywaters
Abbot Jackson Carnes
Ann Cavanaugh
Gill Christian
John Robert Christian
Kate Christian
Meg and John Christian
Penny Turpin Clarke
Hunter Clarkson
Carol Lamb Clifford

Elizabeth and Andrew Cloud
Lucy Ellen Cooley
Neva Corbin
Jill Craddock
Martha Belle Crawford
Anne Creed
Caroline and Bill Crosswell
Jane Cunningham
Verd and Steve Cunningham
Verd Anna Cunningham
Susan Dabbs
Betty and John Davis
Bill and Irma Davis
Cody Davis
Debbie and Jay Davis
Jackie and Sam Davis
Joseph Davis
Laurie and David Davis
Cindy and Pete Dempsey
Scott Derks
Betty Derrick
Barbara Devetski
Leslie Devilier
Gina Dickerson
Gwen and David Diehl
Justin Diehl
Robert Diehl
Angela Dina
Andrea Duncan
Ginger Duncan
Ian Duncan
Bob Eggleston
Sarah Belser Eggleston
Charles Elliott
Duncan Ellison
Eleanor and Gill Ellison
Will Ellison
Angela and Lee Enyart
Mary Heath H. Etheredge
Mary Elizabeth Winfrey Evans
Mikell Fairey
Robert Fairey
Sally and Andy Fairey
Connie Flatten
Charles B. Flowers
Chris and Charles Flowers
Elise and Charlie Flowers
Garrett Flowers
Samantha Flowers
Casey Ford
Jaunea Ford
Bryce Fraser
Evan Fraser
Elizabeth Garrison
Patrick Garrison
Julia Gary
Judy Gass
Catherine Gent

Elizabeth Smiley Glasbrenner
Jan and Bill Glazner
Caroline and Marshall Graham
Karlyn Greenberg
Alan Griffiths
Betsy Haas
Laura Haas
Blair Hamilton
Bonnie and Drew Hamilton
Kim and Andy Hamilton
Carol Hand
Chad Hardaway
Tracy Timmons Hardaway
Frank Harden
Inger Harris
Joan and Herky Harris
Wink Harris
Heyward Harvin
Jeanette Harvin
Ladson Harvin
Maria Harvin
Stewart Harvin IV
John Hayes
Mary and Craig Hayes
Ashlyn Herd
Jenny Herd
Barbara Hollis
Katherine May Hopkins
Tate Horton
Becky Davis Huber
Dawn and David Hunt
Lennon Hunt
Robert Jackson
Meggan McGee Jamison
Stephanie Jamison
Rebecca Johnson
Jeanette Jordan
Mary Junker
Dotty Kolb
Rebecca Kolb
Sally Kolb
Wade Kolb III
Evalina Kuehn
Lloyd LaBadie
Sally LaBadie
Betty Lamb
Sarah Lamb
Susalee and Bill Lamb
William Lamb
Rob Lance
Justina Lasley
Connor Law
Ellen Law
Kristin Leard
Amy Lee
Campbell Lee
Will Lee
Caroline Leggett

Celia Leggett
Christen Leggett
Abigail Lewis
Catherine Lewis
Cricket and Randy Lewis
Eric Lewis
James Lewis
Robin Lewis
Susan Lewis
Patricia Lind
John David Lumpkin
Melissa Lumpkin
Susan and John Lumpkin
Jessica Linke
Jillian Linke
Lynlee and Joe Linke
Cora Sue Mach
Missie and Dan McCarty
Molly McCarty
Scott McCarty
Sharon and Gene McClure
Nellie McCright
Callie McDowell
Carrie and Jeff McDowell
Kara Bateman McDuffie
Kate McKemie
Missi McMorries
Ann Marie and Martin McNamara
Laura McWilliams
Patty Mahlstedt
Frances Martin
Margaret Mathis
Emma Mattson
Trey Mattson
Wendy and Eric Mattson
Mollie Merrick
Eunice and Randy Meyer
Travis Meyer
Christy Mobley
Ann Montgomery
Leonora Montgomery
Anna Bacon Moore
Betsy Moore
Ann Muir
Christie Mullen
Michael Murphey
Morgan Murphey
Susan and Mike Murphey
Virginia Burrows Murray
Betsy and Steve Nelson
Molly McCue Nimmons
Austin Newman
Cricket and Jamie Newman
James Newman
Mica Nixon
Jenny O'Connor
Carol and George O'Day
Christina Oliver

Gail Pace
Mabel Paulus
Greg Pearce
Katherine Pearson and Jim Pfaffman
Juanita Pitts
Abigail Poe
Lasley Poe
Rives Poe
Elizabeth and John Poindexter
Katherine Poindexter
Robert Poindexter
Katina Potinkes
Diane Pryor
Katheryn and Hugh Ray
Mary Carol Ray
Mary Katherine Rebentishch
Derek Redwine
Miriam Reeder
Emily Dransfield Reitz
Janet Roberts
Margaret Robinson
Beth and Robert Rodriguez
Maddie Rodriguez
Sophie Rodriguez
Laura and Stephen Ryan
Sarah Ross
Liza Sansbury
Trish McGehee Sargent
Allison Saunders
Lauren Serebrenik
Nancy and Peter Serebrenik
Zach Serebrenik
Helen Shaffer
Bryant Shelley
James Shelley
Ashley Craddock Shull
Gerry and Jimmy Skardon
Sally Skardon
Louise Slater
Susan Campbell Smith
Beth and Jed Sorensen
Alice Barron Stewart
Bob Stewart
Kathryn Egan Stout
Marilyn Stradtman
Diane Strong
Samantha Sullivan
Janet Roberson Sumner
Cameron Taber
Gail Taber
Carson and Andrew Tate
Mac Tezak
Mary Eleanor Tezak
Sam Tezak
Ansley Tharpe
Carter Tharpe
Laurie and Ed Tharpe
Gale and Bill Thompson

William Richardson Timmons, Jr.
Ellie Towns
Josie Towns
Laurie and Bo Towns
Reid Towns
Tanner Towns
Mary Trainer
Katherine and Bill Turner
Meredith Lind Turner
Betty and Jess Tutor
Katherine Tutor
Kimberly and Brooks Tutor
Sherida Tutor
Clayton Vermeire
Jackie Vermeire
Libby and Brad Vermeire
Katie Waggoner
Carolyn Ann and Mark Walgren
Ellen Walgren
Judy Walgren
Kay and Ken Walgren
Laura Walgren
Anne West
Becki West
Brannon West
Fletcher West
Georgia West
Glenn West
Grace West
John West
Marsie West
Matthew West
Nicolas West
Paige West
Vicki West
Warren West
Warren West III
Sidney Westley
Elizabeth and Ford Wheeler
Burton White
Campbell White
Dennis White
Jill and Togar White
Linden and Cason White
Ridley Wills
Phillip Winfrey
Sally and James Winfrey
Travis Winfrey
Harry Wolfe
Jacob Wood
Judy Wood
Christie Woodfin
Dotty Harris Zarworsky
Jenny and Steve Zimmerly

My Ideas!

My Ideas!

My Ideas!